There is no singular institution as crucial to the health and future well-being of our nation as the family unit. It's God's chosen vehicle for passing on our values, our faith, and our culture, which is exactly why far-Left ideologues laid siege to it for generations. The family is our nation's salvation. Its degradation will be our downfall. Dr. Ben Carson does not mince words; we are in a perilous fight to restore faith, morality, and community in this country. This undertaking can only be achieved if the American family is saved.

CHARLIE KIRK

Faith and family are fundamental pillars of America's success story. As a mother of three, I am encouraged when I see leaders like Dr. Ben Carson fighting to preserve these core values for my children's future. Every American needs a copy of *The Perilous Fight* on their nightstand.

GOVERNOR SARAH HUCKABEE SANDERS

Dr. Ben Carson is a godly man and an effective leader, and he has hit the nail on the head in *The Perilous Fight*. If this country is going to make it, we need to love God and love each other. We need a revival of faith and family. We encourage every American to read this important book.

PHIL and MISS KAY ROBERTSON

The only way we can flourish as a nation and as a society is by embracing faith and family. God bless Dr. Carson for these important words that our country needs to hear and put into practice.

DR. ROBERT JEFFRESS

Dr. Ben Carson's presidential campaign gave those who were paying attention a glimpse of what it might be like to have a decent man run the country. This book spells it out. Reading it is well worth your time.

TUCKER CARLSON

Faith and the family are critical to freedom and the American way of life. And they are currently under attack in this country like we've never seen before. That's why this book from my friend Dr. Ben Carson is so critical. *The Perilous Fight* provides a much-needed conservative road map on how to fight back against the destruction of these critical institutions.

CONGRESSMAN CHIP ROY (R-TX 21

When I think of the American Dream, I think of Dr. Ben Carson. He grew up in poverty, was raised by a single mother from the age of eight on, and went on to receive the Presidential Medal of Freedom in 2008. He has been through a perilous fight and has won. He is a husband, father, grandfather, leader, and shining example of the successes a life of faith and devotion can bring you. I can think of few men more qualified in this country to craft a blueprint for saving the American family.

CANDACE OWENS

I've known Dr. Ben Carson for more than twenty years, and I have great respect for him as a doctor, government leader, and Christian brother. I appreciate the strong stand he takes for families, homes, and the authority of God's Word—all of which are foundational pillars of America that have been under attack. His thought-provoking book lays out how the erosion of religious beliefs has impacted our nation's way of life and what we can do to turn things around. *The Perilous Fight*'s timely message will capture your attention and stir your heart.

FRANKLIN GRAHAM

The road to resolving many of our nation's most pressing issues begins with restoring two of our cornerstone principles—faith and family. I commend my friend Dr. Ben Carson for being a thought leader in this pivotal space at such a crucial moment in American history.

NEWT GINGRICH, former Speaker of the United
States House of Representatives

In this empowering book, Dr. Ben Carson emphasizes reconciliation and unity. He offers a path forward that encourages critical thinking and mature discussion. Even better, you'll discover solutions that benefit our nation's families. Don't wait. Grab a book today and join the movement for the American family.

GOVERNOR MIKE HUCKABEE

Faith and family play a crucial role in the fabric of our nation. Today, we must embrace these values again to avoid damaging and lasting effects. Dr. Carson's new book is a must-read for those who wish to reverse course.

DR. ALVEDA C. KING, Speak for Life

The traditional family is the bedrock of our nation. It's where you learn to respect others, obey your elders, share with others, and embrace the value of hard work. It is important to stand strong against the woke cultural tide at work to water down the importance of the traditional family, and I applaud Dr. Carson for calling attention to this issue.

CONGRESSWOMAN MARY MILLER

Since our nation's founding, the nuclear family structure has allowed families to thrive and overcome hardship and has proved vital to our success as a country. For years now, the Left has attacked the traditional family in an attempt to erode this core foundation. I applaud Dr. Ben Carson for shedding light on this in his new book, *The Perilous Fight*.

PASTOR TONY PERKINS

My friend Dr. Ben Carson provides a captivating and cautionary reminder to us of the importance of preserving faith and family. *The Perilous Fight* delves into why these fundamental principles and values are imperative to our identity as a nation and must be protected.

Former acting attorney general and American Cornerstone
Institute senior fellow MATT WHITAKER

Make no mistake about it, the very idea of the American family is under attack by the radical Left. What they fail to understand is that our embodiment of faith and family is what has made America exceptional. We are in a fight for the soul of this nation, and Dr. Ben Carson has delivered here a well-crafted, conservative battle plan.

SENATOR MIKE LEE

Faith and family have provided the bedrock on which this nation was founded. It is crucial for us to restore these values to the forefront of American culture. I want to thank my friend Dr. Ben Carson for leading the charge. We certainly are in the midst of a perilous fight to defend godly principles and safeguard America as we know it for generations to come.

ELAINE BECK

For years, the Left has criticized faith and family, the very foundational principles that made America a great nation. In *The Perilous Fight*, my friend Dr. Ben Carson brings this important issue to the foreground of American life and culture, offering a hopeful, yet cautionary message to us all.

SENATOR JIM DEMINT

A strong America cannot exist without a society grounded in faith and family. Dr. Ben Carson understands that truth, which is why he is a shining example of the American Dream. Those who feel a sense of urgency to save this nation should read *The Perilous Fight*.

LARA TRUMP

The
PERILOUS
FIGHT

The PERILOUS FIGHT

Overcoming Our Culture's War on the American Family

DR. BEN CARSON

WITH CANDY CARSON

ZONDERVAN BOOKS

ZONDERVAN BOOKS

The Perilous Fight
Copyright © 2024 by Benjamin S. Carson, Sr.

Published in Grand Rapids, Michigan, by Zondervan. Zondervan is a registered trademark of The Zondervan Corporation, L.L.C., a wholly owned subsidiary of HarperCollins Christian Publishing, Inc.

Requests for information should be addressed to customercare@harpercollins.com.

Zondervan titles may be purchased in bulk for educational, business, fundraising, or sales promotional use. For information, please email SpecialMarkets@Zondervan.com.

ISBN 978-0-310-36837-3 (hardcover)
ISBN 978-0-310-36839-7 (audio)
ISBN 978-0-310-36838-0 (ebook)

Unless otherwise noted, Scripture quotations are taken from the New King James Version®. Copyright © 1982 by Thomas Nelson. Used by permission. All rights reserved.

Scripture quotations marked NCV are taken from the New Century Version®. Copyright © 2005 by Thomas Nelson. Used by permission. All rights reserved.

Scripture quotations marked NLT are taken from the Holy Bible, New Living Translation. Copyright © 1996, 2004, 2015 by Tyndale House Foundation. Used by permission of Tyndale House Publishers, Inc., Carol Stream, Illinois 60188. All rights reserved.

Any internet addresses (websites, blogs, etc.) and telephone numbers in this book are offered as a resource. They are not intended in any way to be or imply an endorsement by Zondervan, nor does Zondervan vouch for the content of these sites and numbers for the life of this book.

Published in association with Yates & Yates, www.yates2.com.

Cover design: Curt Diepenhorst
Flag cover photo: JamesBrey / iStockPhoto
Author cover photo: Jared Cummings
Interior design: Sara Colley

Printed in the United States of America

24 25 26 27 28 LBC 5 4 3 2 1

To the strong traditional families
that provide the solid foundation of our nation
and pave the way to success for future generations

CONTENTS

PROLOGUE

Why is this book necessary? Why should you read it?

In this current crazy world, things seem to be more "out of control" than experienced in a way that ground is gained as a result and benefit of accumulated knowledge and effective strategies developed over the ages. But why is the world out of control? If we humans are learning from past mistakes, why would things be getting worse?

A particularly engaging phrase from our national anthem—*perilous fight*—may seem a bit dramatic today, but the very principles our country was founded on are being challenged in a hugely significant way!

When we think of "ramparts" over which we watch (by definition, ramparts are "defensive walls of a castle or walled city [like a fort!], having a broad top with a walkway"), our southern and northern borders come to mind, where any "walls" (literal and figurative) have limited utility due to policies introduced by the current administration.

In the social climate of the United States, each individual is to be respected and supported, in accordance with the Declaration of Independence in which the Founding Fathers wrote that "all men are created equal." That, coupled with an underlying belief that each person, with their unique life experience, brings something special to the table, made our fledgling nation exceptional.

This practice of respecting the ideas and personhood of each human being is one of the reasons our country rose from infancy to worldwide significance in its first fifty years of existence! This was done by combining the best ideas of everyone and building on them. The "newbie" American country that was building its new infrastructure was competing on nearly every level with most well-established nations that had been in existence for centuries!

These unique individuals with their varied life experiences became who they were through a special God-created and God-ordained unit in our country for more than two centuries—a unit mentioned in the very first chapter of the inspired book our Founding Founders based its government on and lived their lives by—*the family*:

> "So God created human beings in his own image.
>   In the image of God he created them;
>   male and female he created them.
>
> "Then God blessed them and said, 'Be fruitful and multiply. Fill the earth and govern it. Reign over the fish in the sea, the birds in the sky, and all the animals that scurry along the ground.'" (Genesis 1:27–28 NLT)

And within that family, there are certain guidelines to follow. In Proverbs 22:6, for example, we are charged, "Direct your children onto the right path, and when they are older, they will not leave it" (NLT), or as we see it in another translation, "Train children to live the right way, and when they are old, they will not stray from it" (NCV). Our God says this about our future: "'For I know the plans I have for you,' says the Lord. 'They are plans for good and not for disaster, to give you a future and a hope'" (Jeremiah 29:11 NLT).

You've most likely heard the saying, "The most successful leaders lead by example." God, our Creator, is not a solo act, although He surely could do everything on His own—He is God, after all! But think about this. God is a triune God—one God, three persons—Father, Son, and Holy Spirit. In His infinite wisdom as Almighty God, He chose to model the human family after His threefold relationship: "Then God said, 'Let *us* make human beings in *our* image" (Genesis 1:26 NLT, emphasis added). In the Garden of Eden, God could have stopped at the creation of Adam. But He didn't. He created male and female.

Fast-forward to modern times. It is not only in America that family is considered important. Other countries have reached the same conclusion. In Great Britain, for example, the Centre for Social Justice stated in a report directed to policymakers, "We need to address our reluctance to talk about the role of family in policy making and government spending if we are to address 'the root causes of poverty.'" Their research findings revealed "the significant relationship between family breakdown and some of the most complex and challenging social issues facing Britain today."[1]

The report notes the dire consequences for those aged eighteen or younger who experience family breakdown.

- They are over twice as likely (2.3 times) to experience homelessness.
- They are twice as likely (2.0 times) to be in trouble with the police or spend time in prison.
- They are almost twice as likely (1.9 times) to experience educational underachievement.
- They are approaching twice as likely (1.8 times) to experience alcoholism.
- They are approaching twice as likely (1.7 times) to experience teen pregnancy.
- They are approaching twice as likely (1.7 times) to experience mental health issues.

- They are more likely (1.6 times) to experience debt.
- They are more likely (1.4 times) to experience being on benefits.[2]

As he toured the world in 1986, Pope John Paul II shared these words in Perth, Australia: "As the family goes, so goes the nation, and so goes the entire world in which we live."[3] The family is indeed the building block for society. Even the United Nations realized this. The family was first formally recognized as having special status in 1989 by the United Nations General Assembly "when it passed resolution A/44/82 (1989) proclaiming 1994 as the first International Year of the Family."[4]

The sad truth is that certain people in other parts of the world understand this "family as building block" reality, desire the successes Americans have and want to control us and our hard-earned resources, and in doing so, are determined to take away our freedoms. Realizing the difficulty of achieving this goal militarily, they have been focusing on ways to destroy us from within, utilizing as one of their strategies the weakening of our families.

W. Cleon Skousen, who wrote *The Naked Communist* (published in 1958), summarizes an idea of world domination by a single governing body as a primary goal. He shared an outline of the "forty-five goals to destroy the United States of America" if this concept were to be implemented in the United States. These goals were presented to the United States Congress during a hearing in 1963, and they will be examined more thoroughly in chapter 4.

Some of the goals target the family specifically:

#40: "Discredit the family as an institution. Encourage promiscuity and easy divorce."

#41: "Emphasize the need to raise children away from the negative influence of parents. Attribute prejudices, mental blocks, and retarding of children to suppressive influence of parents."

Even some of the policies enacted by our own federal government encourage the breakdown of the traditional family. Take, for example, the issue of welfare, where individuals are penalized when another wage earner joins the household.

But knowledge is power. As the old saying goes, "A person forewarned is a person forearmed." This book has been written because the attack on the American family has been under the radar for too long! We need to fight for our country when it's being attacked in any way, shape, or form. And this insidious method is alarming to say the least, and sadly, it has been quite effective. When you read in chapter 4 the entire list of the goals noted by W. Cleon Skousen in his book, you'll see that many of them have already been accomplished over the decades.

As you read this book, it is my hope and prayer that we will be encouraged and be watchful as we work together to help preserve a human institution intended to bless this nation and the people of this nation with a strong and wonderful foundation.

Candy Carson

INTRODUCTION

I t seemed as though mother earth had opened and was vomiting shot
and shell in a sheet of fire and brimstone," wrote Francis Scott Key.[1]
He was describing the long night of September 13, 1814, near the end of
the War of 1812.

That war often gets lost in the shuffle of American history, so a bit
of context may be helpful. Just thirty years after the Revolutionary War,
American interests and British interests were once again in conflict.
Because Britain was locked in a bitter war with Napoleon's France, it
used its naval might to restrict trade routes across the Atlantic. Those
restrictions were harmful to America's desire for economic growth and
geographic expansion.

Particularly galling was the Royal Navy's practice of "impressment,"
in which English officers removed American seamen from their ships and
forced them to serve on British vessels. Such tactics were an outrage for a
young nation seeking respect on the international stage.

For those reasons and more, the United States of America declared
war against Great Britain in June 1812.

Early on, the war effort was a relative success. America won several
naval skirmishes against the British fleet but experienced mixed results in

a number of ground engagements with royal troops stationed in Canada. Then in 1814, American prospects became more desperate when Britain concluded its war with France and turned the greater force of its attention back to the new world.

In August of that year, British forces defeated American defenses at the Battle of Bladensburg, which took place outside Washington D.C. Sensing danger, both military and government officials evacuated the city, including President James Madison. British soldiers entered Washington unopposed, setting aflame the White House, the Capitol, and other federal buildings. A disaster for the young nation.

Right now you might be wondering, *Why the history lesson, Dr. Carson?* That's a fair question. The answer is that I want to make sure you understand the peril faced by the United States and its people in that moment. Remember, America had only been a sovereign nation for a little over thirty years. It was an infant when set against the scale of history, especially in comparison with an empire as old and as powerful as Great Britain.

Imagine you had been an American citizen in that moment. You would have kept track of the war over the past couple years and would not have been encouraged. Victories always seemed paired with defeats. The threat of the enemy grew greater every week. Then you would have heard the shocking news that Washington had been overrun. The White House and the Capitol were ablaze. President Madison and all the members of his cabinet had fled, and there seemed little hope of stopping the British advance.

That was the reality when Francis Scott Key boarded a British naval vessel in September 1814. An attorney by trade, Key had come to appeal for the freedom of his friend, whom the British had wrongly imprisoned on their ship. Key won that appeal, but he and his friend were detained temporarily because the British fleet planned to attack the port of Baltimore and would not allow anyone to raise the alarm in advance.

This was a critical moment—maybe *the* critical moment. Baltimore was a major point of access for both the American military and civilian merchants. If that port were to fall into enemy hands, America's hopes for winning the war would be bleak indeed. If America's defenses could hold, there would yet be hope for future victories. Yet another defeat could mean more than a war was lost.

The promise of America itself was in danger.

With a heavy heart, Key and his friend were forced to watch from off-shore as the assault on Baltimore began. Twenty British ships bombarded Fort McHenry from the Baltimore harbor, sending volley after volley of rockets and mortar shells. The attack continued for more than twenty-five hours, with missiles blazing continually through the night and into the morning of September 14.

It was on that morning when Key witnessed a huge American flag flying over the fort at the hour of reveille. The attack had been repelled. The harbor remained open. The Battle of Baltimore became a rallying victory for the United States, leading to similar triumphs in New York and New Orleans—and ultimately to the end of the war.

Still aboard the enemy vessel on that fateful morning, Francis Scott Key wrote the first draft of an anthem that has inspired millions of his fellow citizens in recent centuries:

> *O say can you see, by the dawn's early light,*
> *What so proudly we hail'd at the twilight's last gleaming,*
> *Whose broad stripes and bright stars through the perilous fight*
> *O'er the ramparts we watch'd were so gallantly streaming?*
> *And the rocket's red glare, the bombs bursting in air,*
> *Gave proof through the night that our flag was still there,*
> *O say does that star-spangled banner yet wave*
> *O'er the land of the free and the home of the brave?*

The perilous fight—those words arrest my attention whenever I place my right hand over my heart and face the flag at the playing of our national anthem. They are a reminder that America was born in a crucible of fire. Freedom was not given freely but had to be fought for and defended.

There is another war currently underway that threatens the vital values and ideals on which America was founded—another perilous fight. As in the days of 1814, the fate of America hangs in the balance of this war. Our nation hangs in the balance. Our sovereignty. We are facing an enemy who wishes to destroy us, not with rockets, bombs, or ballistics of any kind, but from within.

As was the case at the Battle of Baltimore, this war for America's soul has narrowed to a specific field of engagement. Not Fort McHenry this time. Rather, the American family is under heavy bombardment and sustained attack. Our enemies have been chipping away at their target for decades, and they now believe the time is right for a full-scale assault.

Who will win this perilous fight? The answer is unclear. Yet as I will show in the pages that follow, the stakes could not be higher.

My Story So Far

Back when I was a younger man, if you would have told me I would become an advocate for the traditional American family, I would have politely questioned your sanity. After all, I'm not the product of a traditional family. My father left our home when my brother and I were still young. We rarely saw him. Thankfully, my mother is a strong woman who did everything she could to make life better for her kids, even in conditions that were far from ideal.

Because of her wisdom, hard work, and dogged determination—coupled with regular contributions from a few positive male role models—my brother and I entered into adulthood on relatively firm footing. In fact, in many ways my life is an embodiment of the American dream.

My specific dream from a young age was to become a doctor, which for someone like me from a nontraditional family from inner-city Detroit, was scoffed at by many. But much to their surprise—and mine—I made it. Having learned the value of education through my mother's relentless repetition, I earned a scholarship to Yale University and then continued on at the University of Michigan and Johns Hopkins University Medical School. I spent years enjoying a storied career as a pediatric neurosurgeon. I was awarded the Presidential Medal of Freedom, the highest civilian honor available in our nation, and was named one of eighty-nine "living legends" by the Library of Congress on its two hundredth anniversary. I have received more than seventy honorary doctorate degrees.

These and other accolades have certainly been appreciated. Without the unique opportunities I have been afforded through the wonderful expression of freedom that defines America, I don't know where I may have ended up. The road to success surely would have been much more difficult.

So, no, I did not experience the benefits of a traditional American family in the early portions of my life. But I have enjoyed those benefits in later years, first as a husband and then as father and grandfather. My wife, Candy, and I have witnessed firsthand the wonders of true collaboration in our marriage—a partnership in which both parties win. And we remain in awe of the incredible privilege and responsibility embedded in doing life with our children and intentionally imparting our values to them.

I fully intended to retire from stress and strain when I stepped away from my medical practice. Of course I had interests I still wanted to pursue, including travel and recreation, but I thought the remainder of my life would be quietly focused on the joys of being a husband, a father, and a grandfather. Yet having discovered the priceless nature of the nuclear family, I found myself pulled into fields that were utterly foreign to my early life. I began writing books on social issues and speaking out on behalf of the home that has been such a gift to me.

That is why I entered the political arena. I wanted others to experience that same gift! And I already saw that the gift of family was under threat.

I'll never forget the first debate of the 2016 presidential primaries. I was well-versed in public speaking by that point, but this was a different level. The heat of the lights. The buzz of the audience. The weight of knowing that the world was watching.

There were moments leading up to that night when I wondered, *Why am I here?* But I knew the answer: for my family, and for families in general.

I didn't run for president because I desired the power or prestige of the presidency. Far from it! I took my place on that debate stage because I was determined to fight for American families. Even in those days, the assault against the traditional family had reached a level of intensity and vitriol that shocked me. I knew someone had to stand up for families, and so I threw my hat into the ring.

I had a chance to speak with Donald Trump after the final Republican debate, and I shared a conviction that had been growing in my mind.

"You're going to be the next president," I told him.

He looked surprised to hear that from one of his rivals. "Why do you say that?" he asked.

"Because God's not finished with this country yet," I answered. "And He has work for you to do." A big part of that work, I believed then and still believe now, was to shore up and support American families.

Though I failed to win the nomination, Donald Trump won the presidency. I had the privilege of serving as Secretary of the Department of Housing and Urban Development. My time in that role underscored the dangers facing families in the modern world—especially those families seeking to maintain the Judeo-Christian ethic in an increasingly hostile culture. I'm deeply grateful for the team we put together at HUD, and I am especially proud of the work we did to protect American families.

After my time in government, I once again fully intended to retire. But once more, my retirement failed. I quickly realized I would never be able to play golf or go on cruises around the world while watching my beloved nation deteriorate.

Therefore, I launched the American Cornerstone Institute—what I call a "think tank / do tank"—in order to continue this perilous fight. Our goal at ACI is to strengthen the bonds of our communities by lifting up the virtues of faith, liberty, community, and life. These are the cornerstone principles essential to the success of our nation—principles that can be bolstered immeasurably and immediately by strengthening our families.

That is my goal for this book.

My Purpose for This Book

Candy and I have been privileged to visit sixty-eight countries and to live overseas in various seasons of our lives, and we've gained an interesting perspective on how the world views our United States. For the most part, that view remains quite positive.

Yes, some people view America as an evil nation and a root cause of many of the problems that currently exist in the world. Surprisingly (and quite sadly), many who think that way are themselves American citizens! Yet having witnessed much of the world firsthand, I vehemently oppose such a view. In fact, I can say with confidence that America remains the greatest nation and civilization the world has ever seen.

As I travel to other regions and other nations, I continually encounter those who admire and aspire to the American dream of freedom, equality, and opportunity for all. Indeed, that dream shines in the hearts of millions of souls every year who are willing to risk everything—often including their lives—in order to reach these shores.

The American dream remains incredibly powerful. At the same time, our American society is no doubt in decline.

An important research project measured the progress of more than 160 nations for many years, focusing on hard data to measure overall quality of life. Those data points include nutrition, safety, freedom, environmental impact, physical health, access to healthcare, education, and much more.

During the period between 2011 and 2020, 160 of the nations measured by that research project advanced in their scores. Only three nations declined in terms of the overall well-being of their citizens—Brazil, Hungary, and the United States. Among those three, Americans experienced the steepest level of decline.[2]

The data paints an alarming picture for the United States, which now ranks twenty-eighth in terms of overall well-being for its citizens, behind such rivals as Estonia, the Czech Republic, and Cyprus. The data paints a confusing picture as well. America ranks first in the world in terms of the quality of its universities, yet ninety-first when measuring access to quality basic education. Similarly, we are at the cutting edge of medical technology, ahead of all other nations—yet US citizens are ninety-seventh in terms of access to quality healthcare. Importantly, these figures predated the COVID pandemic.[3]

Responding to that study, economist David Blanchflower noted, "Rising distress and despair are largely American phenomenon not observed in other advanced countries."[4] Our global influence is waning; strife in our nation is increasing; and we are seeing ideologically driven political hatred at levels not seen since the Civil War—hatred that seems to preclude logic and common sense.

What happened? Is America in decline because of the complex challenges that have arisen around the world?

No. The early days of our nation—the days of Francis Scott Key, James Madison, Thomas Jefferson, George Washington, and so many others—were filled with challenges, and yet those challenges became the crucible that fueled America's steep rise from international obscurity to an industrial force to be reckoned with, and ultimately to the world's major global superpower, all in a relatively short span of time. Similarly, the challenges of world wars and ideological discord that defined the twentieth century could not crush the American spirit.

The premise of this book is that America is not simply experiencing decline; we are under attack. In fact, we have been under attack for decades. Our enemies seek our destruction, but not through traditional warfare. Instead, they have used corrosion and corruption to destroy us from within.

You've felt the effects of that corrosion, haven't you? You sense the hostility that has crept into American life. You perceive the growing tension in your community, in the workplace, and even at home. You see the refusal to tolerate any way of thinking that does not line up with the specific worldviews that are accepted and expected.

Importantly, this attack against America is being waged on two primary fronts—faith and family. I'll have much to say within these pages about the importance of faith and the necessary role it has played (and must continue to play) in our culture. However, the primary focus of this book will be the brutal, unceasing, and deadly assault currently being waged against American families—especially the traditional nuclear family.

Have you noticed the ways this attack has expanded in recent years? Traditional families are increasingly mocked by the entertainment industry as antiquated and unnecessary. Fathers in movies and TV shows have been reduced to arrogant dolts who offer nothing to their loved ones. Mothers have been assigned the impossible task of maintaining a stellar career and a perfect home. Parents' rights are constantly undermined by the educational system. What used to be considered "alternative lifestyles" are now lifted up as preferred expressions for gender and sexuality. To question these developments is to risk being accused of hatred and bigotry.

In short, so much that feels deeply wrong has been elevated as acutely right, and it may seem like there's nothing we can do about it. Thankfully, though, we are neither helpless nor hopeless!

In the chapters that follow, we will:

+ Explore the original boundaries set around families by our Creator, and the benefits those boundaries offer to both the home and the community.
+ Highlight specific ways that American families are under fire, exposing the threat and displaying the danger.
+ Lay out specific, practical ways we can join together and engage in the perilous fight to rejuvenate America by saving American families.

Are you ready to engage in this perilous fight? Are you ready to stand for your family and all families in our great nation? Then let us continue forward together.

ONE

A

GREAT

DESIGN

If there's any cereal left, it's mine. You ate two bowls yesterday all by your—"

I had been talking with my brother, Curtis, early on a Sunday morning when we walked into the kitchen. As soon as we made it through the door, however, all conversation stopped. All thoughts of breakfast stopped. Really, all thoughts of any kind came to a halt because we saw something we never expected to see.

Money. Lots of money.

Curtis and I saw our parents seated at the kitchen table, their heads down and brows furrowed. On the table in front of them were stacks of currency. There were dollar bills, fives, tens, twenties—I think I even saw a hundred-dollar bill sitting by itself, somewhat hidden among the rows of green paper. It was more than all the money I had seen up to that point in my life put together. Far more.

"What are you . . .?"

"Where did you . . .?"

Of course, Curtis and I both erupted with questions once the initial shock wore off, but our words were silenced when Mom held up her finger without looking up. That gesture meant "Be quiet," and we both knew the consequences of violating the command. Still dumbfounded, we watched as she meticulously counted the bills into stacks and recorded the amounts on a small legal pad.

When she finished, she told us there was almost $8,000 sitting on our kitchen table—the equivalent of about $80,000 in today's valuation.

"Boys," she finally told us, "this money is for the mortgage. We're going to use it to pay off the house."

We had a long talk about money that Sunday morning in our kitchen. Mom told us about the importance of working hard, the value of being thrifty and spending less than we earned, and the need to have a plan for saving a little bit of every paycheck in order to provide for the future. I don't know about Curtis, but the presence of all that money kept me focused on every word she said. She had my full attention!

My dad was present during that experience, but he didn't contribute much in terms of financial wisdom. In fact, I remember his face looking bewildered more than anything else. Later, Curtis and I learned that Mom saved all that money in secret so Dad didn't waste it. We also discovered that Mom fully recognized the extent of her husband's failures in that moment, and that her determination to pay off the mortgage was in some part based on their imminent divorce—and her knowledge that she would likely get the house in the settlement.

Our financial situation took a turn for the worse when the divorce was finalized. Despite her fierce determination, Sonya Carson was still an uneducated single mother who worked two or three jobs at a time in order to keep our heads above water. Even so, knowing that my mother had successfully saved so much money gave me a sense of calm assurance that carried me through even our most severe financial storms.

In many ways, I am writing this book in defense of something I never experienced as a child or teen—a strong traditional family. It sounds strange, but that Sunday morning watching my mother count stacks of cash may be the fondest memory I can recall with all four members of my family in the same room—Mom, Dad, Curtis, and me. Once Dad left the picture, he remained out of the picture for the remainder of his life. I'll share a bit more about our family's experience in the last section of this chapter.

Thankfully, I had the opportunity to establish a strong family of my own when I met and married Candy, the love of my life. The memory of my own childhood lack was a huge motivation for doing things well as we raised our own children and established our own family bonds.

Now, what do I mean by a "traditional" family, or what is often called a "nuclear" family? The most basic definition would be a family unit comprised of two married parents and their biological or adoptive children. This is distinct from a "blended" family in which one or both parents have children with other partners. It is also distinct from families where the parents live together but are not married, or where a single parent raises children on his or her own.

For the vast majority of human history, traditional families have served as the basic building blocks of communities and societies.

The Significance of the Family

Imagine a room filled with one hundred teens. Let's say these teens are thirteen or fourteen years old and relatively well-behaved. Imagine your own children (or grandchildren) in that room, along with nieces, nephews, and cousins. Think of the children you encounter in your community and at church—those who come to your home each Halloween seeking candy.

This is a diverse group of teens. Half are young women and half are young men, just as we see in America at large. They are White, Black, Hispanic, Asian, Native American, and more. Some are short, while others are tall. Some are dressed nicely in expensive clothes and shoes, while others wear threadbare shirts and out-of-style jeans. Many are a bit round, and some are beanpole thin. Most are somewhere in between.

These teens are all seated at desks arranged in rows, and they are all looking forward—all looking at you.

Can you see them? Take a moment to close your eyes and picture their faces. Curious. Hopeful. Both excited for the future and uncertain about what lies ahead.

Now, what if you had the power to guide those teens toward three choices that would all but guarantee economic safety and security in their adult lives? Meaning, if every teen in that room were to make those three choices, then ninety-eight of them would never experience poverty as adults. The vast majority would make it to the middle class and have the opportunity to rise even higher if they desired.

What would you do if I was able to give you the authority to make that happen?

You would jump at the opportunity, of course! You wouldn't even need to think about it. Three simple steps to guarantee that 98 percent of those children never experience poverty? It's a no-brainer. Also, of course, you would rightly do everything in your power to support those two teens who slipped through the cracks. With the vast majority of the group on the track toward prosperity, you would be free to concentrate your humanitarian efforts and your compassion on the small minority who need some extra assistance.

Have you guessed where I'm going with this? The situation I've just described is not hypothetical; it's real. And it reveals the very real value of the nuclear family.

Several years ago, the Brookings Institution—a prestigious and well-funded research organization—reported on the findings from a large-scale study of poverty in the United States. The researchers made an astonishing discovery: 98 percent of American teens who take three simple steps are able to avoid poverty as adults.

What are those three steps?

1. Complete at least a high school education.
2. Get a full-time job.
3. Wait until after marriage to have children.[1]

In other words, young people can greatly increase their chances for economic prosperity if they pursue a traditional approach to growing up and starting a family. Similarly, parents can greatly increase the chances of their children experiencing success in life if they steer those children toward the three steps listed above.

More recently, the Brookings Institution partnered with Princeton University on a report titled "Strong Families, Prosperous States: Do Healthy Families Affect the Wealth of States?" As you can see from the title, that report focused, not on individuals or even individual families, but on how the well-being of families impacts entire states.

The findings were eye-opening, to say the least: "Higher levels of marriage, and especially higher levels of married-parent families, are strongly associated with more economic growth, more economic mobility, less child poverty, and higher median family income at the state level in the United States."[2]

States with higher levels of traditional families had:

+ more wealth (higher median family income)
+ more upward mobility (people moving from poverty to wealth)
+ less child poverty
+ much less violent crime[3]

Most recently, Melissa Kearney—the Neil Moskowitz professor of economics at the University of Maryland—wrote a book in 2023 called *The Two-Parent Privilege*. The book offers a deep and detailed exploration of what most cultures have already known for centuries—that children raised outside of a traditional family are more likely to suffer harm of various kinds than those within a traditional family.

In Kearney's words:

I have studied US poverty, inequality, and family structure for almost a quarter of a century. I approach these issues as a hardheaded—albeit softhearted—MIT-trained economist. Based on the overwhelming evidence at hand, I can say with the utmost confidence that the decline in marriage and the corresponding rise in the share of children being raised in one-parent homes has contributed to the economic insecurity of American families, has widened the gap in opportunities and outcomes for children from different backgrounds, and today poses economic and social challenges that we cannot afford to ignore—but may not be able to reverse.[4]

The data is clear. When it comes to raising children and securing the economic foundation of a nation for generations, what we call the traditional nuclear family is the most effective tool for generational success ever devised.

Before we explore why that is the case, there was another detail in Kearney's book that caught my attention:

When I have spoken with other scholars in recent years about my plans to write this book, the most common response I have gotten is along the lines of "I tend to agree with you about all this—but are you sure you want to be out there saying this publicly?" I have thought about that a lot.[5]

We should think about that too. The studies and statistics I have mentioned here are not a secret. They have been publicly available for many years. Even decades. Nor are these the only research projects that highlight the benefits of two-parent families. Educators, economists, and policy makers are all keenly aware that traditional families have a high correlation with producing healthy and successful children.

Yet those same educators, economists, and policymakers—not to mention politicians at the local and federal levels—have done nothing to increase the percentage of children raised in traditional families across recent decades. In fact, many of the laws and policies they have instituted make it more likely for children to be raised *outside* of traditional families. Examples include no-fault divorce, welfare programs that incentivize single-parent households, and laws that make adoption difficult or pro-hibitively expensive for many nuclear families.

Worse, people like Melissa Kearney are often discouraged from even talking about these realities. There is a chilling wind in academia, the media, and government that cuts across many who would otherwise try to support traditional families.

All of that begs the question, "Why?" Why would so many in our nation support a system that makes it *more likely* for younger generations to experience poverty and violent crime, yet *less likely* to benefit from relational stability and social mobility? Why would people be shamed or canceled for attempting to shine a light on that reality?

There is an answer, and we're going to uncover it in a later chapter. For now, let's keep the focus on families.

The Design of the Family

Here's another question worth considering: Why is the traditional nuclear family so successful? Why do families with two married parents raising their own children have a higher proclivity for producing successful adult children than nontraditional families?

A lot of people have offered answers to that question, including these:

+ Two-parent households are more economically efficient and adaptable than single-parent households.
+ Traditional families allow parents to lean on each other and receive support when one of those parents is struggling.
+ Traditional families tend to be more childcentric; the structure of the family is built around children rather than adults.
+ Both boys and girls live with active role models in a two-parent household.

And there are many more examples.

These reasons are valid. They make sense. But they don't tell the whole story. Indeed, I would suggest that these and other attempted explanations are symptoms of the traditional family's success rather than the root cause of that success.

What is the root cause then? The simple reason traditional families are so effective at producing healthy, stable, prosperous human beings is because human beings were *designed* to grow and mature within the context of traditional families. Children thrive in nuclear families for the same reason birds thrive in nests—they were created to do so. We know that because the Creator of human beings—who is also the Creator of the family—laid out the guidelines for families in the Bible, which is His manual for life.

So, before we dig more deeply into the state of families in our world today, and specifically into the state of families in America, I think it's important to take a step back and look at what the family is supposed to be—what it was designed to be and how it was intended to function.

The book of Genesis lays out the descriptive foundation for the family, starting on the very first page:

> So God created man in His own image; in the image of God He created him; male and female He created them. Then God blessed them, and God said to them, "Be fruitful and multiply; fill the earth and subdue it; have dominion over the fish of the sea, over the birds of the air, and over every living thing that moves on the earth." (Genesis 1:27–28)

You'll notice that "male and female He created them" involves a binary, which is not a popular concept in today's world. (More on that later.) But I want to focus for now on the truth that human beings are created "in the image of God." Specifically, that "image" is tied to the binary of "male and female." Adam wasn't created in God's image as a single individual.

Rather, Adam and Eve were created in God's image as two individuals brought together for a purpose: "'Be fruitful and multiply; fill the earth and subdue it.'"

Remember that God exists as a divine community. He is God the Father, God the Son, and God the Spirit—each of those unique Persons exist together in unity. A living relationship.

Humanity is created in God's image because we are intended to function as a similar community. We were created by the community called God to live and thrive as a community of individuals, and that community begins with the family.

We see that theme continued in Genesis 2:18: "And the LORD God said, 'It is not good that man should be alone; I will make him a helper comparable to him.'" The King James Version, which is what I studied growing up and still prefer to read, uses the uncommon word *helpmeet* instead of *helper*. The literal translation for that word is "a helper like himself." It should be noted that God did not take a bone from the foot, signifying that the helper was to be inferior. Nor did He take a piece of the skull to signify that the helper was to be superior. Instead, God created Eve using a rib from Adam's side, indicating the helper would be an equal who would "help meet" the challenges of their future together.

Several verses later, the text reinforces the purpose for that system:

And Adam said:

> "This is now bone of my bones
> And flesh of my flesh;
> She shall be called Woman,
> Because she was taken out of Man."

Therefore a man shall leave his father and mother and be joined to his wife, and they shall become one flesh. (Genesis 2:23–24)

Here is the principle: God designed the family to be the foundation for human life in our world. The family begins with two individuals who are different but equal—a man and a woman. These two join together as "one flesh." They become a living, breathing community meant to enjoy the deepest intimacy: "They were both naked . . . and were not ashamed" (Genesis 2:25).

What is the purpose of such a vibrant, intimate community? As already stated, the purpose is to "be fruitful and multiply." No, procreation is not the only purpose for marriage—but it is *a* purpose. In fact, it is a primary purpose, and one that should never be ignored.

Scripture affirms the necessary role of children within the family:

> Behold, children are a heritage from the LORD,
> The fruit of the womb is a reward.
> Like arrows in the hand of a warrior,
> So are the children of one's youth.
> Happy is the man who has his quiver full of them;
> They shall not be ashamed,
> But shall speak with their enemies in the gate.
>
> (Psalm 127:3–5)

Finally, and critically, the Bible makes it clear that families are designed as permanent institutions. Combining two unique individuals into "one flesh" is not a temporary amalgamation. Marriage is a life-changing, lifelong union between husband and wife.

For that reason, Scripture affirms that divorce was not and is not part of God's plan for families:

> For the LORD God of Israel says
> That He hates divorce,
> For it covers one's garment with violence. (Malachi 2:16)

"Furthermore it has been said, 'Whoever divorces his wife, let him give her a certificate of divorce.' But I say to you that whoever divorces his wife for any reason except sexual immorality causes her to commit adultery; and whoever marries a woman who is divorced commits adultery." (Matthew 5:31–32)

And [Jesus] answered and said to them, "Have you not read that He who made them at the beginning 'made them male and female,' and said, 'For this reason a man shall leave his father and mother and be joined to his wife, and the two shall become one flesh'? So then, they are no longer two but one flesh. Therefore what God has joined together, let not man separate." (Matthew 19:4–6)

Does that mean a woman suffering physical or emotional abuse must be trapped in a harmful marriage? No, there are commonsense instructions given in Scripture about divorce, and we will cover that topic in greater depth in later chapters. But as a principle, God's intention was for the union of husband and wife to be permanent—"till death do us part."

So then, the basic guidelines for families as outlined by our Creator is one man and one woman permanently joined in passion and purpose as one flesh, not for their own fulfillment as individuals, but so that the next generation may also grow and flourish.

That's marriage. That's family. That's the plan given to us by God. And there are harmful consequences for all involved when we deviate from that plan.

Common Objections to the Traditional Family

Nothing I have described in these pages so far is original to me, nor should it be particularly surprising. The family has been the central unit of human life for as long as there has been human life. That reality is affirmed by human experience and the Bible.

These truths were especially meaningful in the earliest days of America as a nation. Our forefathers understood the value of families, which is why they created policies that encouraged and empowered families to flourish. Those families were largely built on the foundation of God's values and God's will as expressed in the Bible, which resulted in a long period of moral clarity and healthy communities.

Some may be shocked to hear me say that. They may ask, "What about slavery? How can you describe people as morally strong if they had slaves?"

The short answer is that slavery was never unique to America. Indeed, even a casual review of human history will reveal that slavery has been part of virtually every human civilization in existence prior to the nineteenth century. The Egyptian pyramids were built by slaves (including the Hebrew people). The Roman Empire bought or captured slaves from all over the world and sold them all over the world. The same is true of the Ottomans and other Asian dynasties. In Africa, strong tribes conquered weaker tribes and turned their people into slaves, which they often sold.

So, no, slavery was not unique to the American economy. Yet America is unique in that so many of its citizens became so morally opposed to slavery that they fought a bloody civil war so as to end that institution. The moral fiber of American families was essential in producing young men willing to give their lives in order to end that evil practice.

People raise several other arguments when it comes to families in the modern world, specifically with establishing the Bible as the primary source of guidance for what families should look like. Many believe the Bible to be antiquated or even harmful in our current culture. Therefore, let's spend a little time addressing some of the major questions often raised.

First, many object to the biblical definition of family on the grounds that many families described in the Bible did not follow that definition. "What about all the families in the Bible that featured multiple wives?"

That is a good question. As we have seen, the Bible was clear from the beginning that God's plan for families was the joining together of one husband and one wife in order to both produce and train up offspring for the next generation. Yet Scripture contains several examples of families that feature one husband with multiple wives—including such notable figures as Abraham, Jacob, David, and Solomon. How can we resolve the tension between those two realities?

The main answer is that the reality of men and women failing to follow God's design does not invalidate the designs. In fact, looking at the lives of the men I just mentioned reveals the dangers associated with polygamy.

What was the result of Abraham's polygamous marriage to Hagar? Strife in his family and generational strife between the descendants of his two sons, Isaac and Ishmael. What caused Jacob's polygamous marriage to both Leah and Rachel? He was deceived; he loved Rachel yet was forced to marry Leah. What was the result of David's pursuit of multiple wives? Adultery and murder with regard to Bathsheba, and constant strife within his household. And what was the result of Solomon's seven hundred wives? A loss of faith that darkened the later years of his life and tarnished his legacy.

In short, the Bible actively reveals God's preference for a family of one husband and one wife who raise their children together. The Bible also passively reveals the harmful consequences that occur when we attempt to build alternate styles of families.

Another common objection to the biblical definition of family centers on the ominous but amorphous threat of "the patriarchy." Many ask, "Doesn't the traditional family elevate men above women?"

The main reason for this line of thinking stems from the biblical concept of the man (husband) as "head" of the family. This principle is stated directly in several Scripture passages, including these:

> But I want you to know that the head of every man is Christ, the head of woman is man, and the head of Christ is God. (1 Corinthians 11:3)

> Wives, submit to your own husbands, as to the Lord. For the husband is head of the wife, as also Christ is head of the church; and He is the Savior of the body. Therefore, just as the church is subject to Christ, so let the wives be to their own husbands in everything. (Ephesians 5:22–24)

It's true that these and other passages have been used in history to suggest that men should take a dominant place over women in general, and that husbands should dominate their wives. It's also true that many individual men have sought to assert themselves in ways that overshadowed their wives, even to the point of physical and emotional abuse.

Let me be clear, any such practices are morally reprehensible and contrary to the Bible's guidelines for families. The husband's role as "head" of the household refers to leadership, not dominance. Scripture makes that crystal clear in many passages, including these:

> Husbands, love your wives, just as Christ also loved the church and gave Himself for her. . . . So husbands ought to love their own wives as their own bodies; he who loves his wife loves himself. (Ephesians 5:25, 28)

> Husbands, likewise, dwell with them with understanding, giving honor to the wife, as to the weaker vessel, and as being heirs together of the grace of life, that your prayers may not be hindered. (1 Peter 3:7)

The biblical design for families is for husbands to actively love and cherish their wives—and even to sacrifice themselves on behalf of their wives in the same way Christ sacrificed Himself for the church. Husbands are to show "understanding" within their families and shower their wives with "honor." Surely these guidelines leave no room for abuse of any kind.

But what about the concept of "headship"? Some would ask, "Why is it necessary for husbands to take a leadership role within the family? Why is it necessary to have a 'head' at all?" This is another important question that deserves an answer.

Imagine a team of explorers was making an expedition deep in the heart of an undeveloped jungle. Because they wanted to be team players, each explorer was given an equal share in the decision-making processes—meaning, there was no single leader, and all decisions were to be discussed, voted on, and enacted unanimously as a group. How long until that team descended into chaos? How effectively would that group navigate emergency situations or life-threatening encounters that required quick thinking and even quicker action?

Or imagine a corporation with dozens of employees governed in the same way—each employee has an equal share in the company, which means each employee has equal authority for making decisions. Those of us who are idealists may believe this sounds like a great plan, and that such a company will function smoothly as a healthy, utopian reality. But those of us who are observers of human nature know the truth: such a company will quickly devolve into factions, squabbles, and turmoil.

My point is this: Just about every organization that involves multiple people naturally and automatically sets up a leadership structure. Why? Because leaders are necessary for moving things forward rather than getting stuck in a quagmire of everybody's opinions. In the same way, every family needs a leader. Not a tyrant, not a bully, but a leader—someone to take charge and take responsibility when necessary.

It's true that many women are better leaders than many men, and it's true that many husbands make boneheaded decisions that harm themselves and their families. But remember, we are talking about the original plan for families as designed by our Creator. That plan calls for husbands and wives to be partners of equal value in the home, planning out their goals and priorities together. But that plan also calls for husbands to assume the responsibility of leadership so that everyone can keep moving forward when the family is deadlocked and decisions need to be made.

A Word to Those in Nontraditional Families

There's a good chance you may be feeling sad or frustrated right now if you are part of a nontraditional family. Maybe your parents got divorced during your childhood. Maybe you are divorced and find yourself a single mom or dad. Maybe you're single when you would rather not be. Maybe your family has been blended in so many ways that it's hard to keep track of who's who.

You may wonder, *Am I excluded from God's blessings or from success in life because my family doesn't fit within God's original design?*

The answer is a resounding no. I'm not telling you anything of the sort. God established His design for the family in the same way He established His design for every facet of our lives. Yet because of the reality of sin in our hearts, we often walk away from those designs. We rebel. We seek our own way and pursue our own goals. Thankfully, God offers grace to us as individuals and grace to our families.

My own experience is a perfect example. My mom got married when she was thirteen years old, taken in by a man in his late twenties who turned out to be a bigamist. He had another family we knew nothing about. That revelation split our home when I was eight years old, and my brother and I rarely saw our father again from that point forward.

Of course, that experience left my mom to raise two young sons on her own, and she did everything she could to provide for our needs. She worked three jobs. She offered love when we needed love, and discipline when we needed a kick in the pants. She was wise and kind. Having never finished grade school, she hammered home the value of education and pressed us to take our studies seriously. In so many ways, our mom was the center of the world for Curtis and me. To this day, there is no person I respect more.

Yet our situation was hard on her—and on us. I wondered so often what it would be like to have a father in our home. Someone to wrestle with. Someone to teach me all the things I wanted to learn. Someone to show me what it meant to be a man.

All families are sources of blessings and pain. My goal in this chapter is not to suggest that some families are doing things "right" and others are doing things "wrong." Instead, I'm highlighting God's design for the family so we can join together in celebrating what is currently working well regarding that design—and in highlighting the ways our culture has drifted away from it.

In the end, what we call the traditional or nuclear family is not a relic from the *Leave It to Beaver* days of the 1950s and '60s. It's not an antiquated notion that should be abandoned along with lead paint or cigarettes in hospital delivery rooms.

The traditional family is a gift that has blessed America and empowered our citizens, and that gift is in danger. It is under attack.

It must be defended.

TWO

COMMUNITY, CULTURE, NATION

Are you familiar with John Muir? You won't find his face on many monuments, yet filmmaker Ken Burns says Muir "ascended to the pantheon of the highest individuals in our country; I'm talking about the level of Abraham Lincoln, and Martin Luther King, and Thomas Jefferson, and Elizabeth Cady Stanton, Jackie Robinson—people who have had a transformational effect on who we are."[1]

In many ways, John Muir was a living embodiment of the American Dream, even though his story began outside of America.

Born in Scotland in 1838, Muir emigrated to America at the age of eleven and settled with his family near Portage, Wisconsin. The Muirs were farmers, and John learned the family trade at an early age. But he was also an inventor. He developed working clocks made entirely from wood and even developed a device that tipped him out of bed before dawn.

Muir attended the University of Wisconsin but dropped out in order to travel. He spent years working odd jobs throughout the Northern US and Canada. He once walked a thousand miles from Indianapolis to the Gulf of Mexico. He sailed to Cuba, then to Panama, then up the West Coast to San Francisco, where he fell in love—not with a woman, but with the landscape of the Sierra Nevada.

"Then it seemed to me the Sierra should be called [not] the Nevada, or Snowy Range," he wrote, "but the Range of Light . . . the most divinely beautiful of all the mountain chains I have ever seen."[2] He took up a flock of sheep and became a shepherd in the Yosemite Valley.

Eventually, Muir did marry a woman named Louie Wanda

Strentzel. They managed a fruit orchard together and raised two daughters. But John never lost his passion for the transformational power of nature. "Everybody needs beauty as well as bread," he wrote, "places to play in and pray in, where nature may heal and give strength to body and soul alike."[3]

Firm in that belief, Muir spent the rest of his life working to conserve and protect many of America's most pristine landscapes. His work as a writer and activist played a primary role in the creation of Yosemite National Park through an act of Congress. Other parks soon followed at Sequoia, Mount Rainier, the Petrified Forest, and the Grand Canyon. Later, Muir founded and ran the Sierra Club in order "to do something for wildness and make the mountains glad."[4]

For these reasons and more, John Muir is known today as the father of the national parks system in America.

Now, think about the timeline and the progression of Muir's story. He came to America as part of a hardworking immigrant family. That hard work paid dividends, and John received access to freedoms and opportunities unavailable to him in his native Scotland—including the chance at a college education. As he grew and matured, Muir raised his own family, contributed greatly to his local community in Northern California, and ultimately became a force that benefited all of the United States.

That's the promise of America in action. More specifically, that's the promise of *American families* in action. Families are the foundational building blocks of our communities, which means that investment in those families produces massive benefits for all.

In today's world, we often mistakenly believe that what takes place within our individual families only impacts our individual families— almost like, "What happens in Vegas stays in Vegas." This is a false assertion. What happens in our families does impact our *families*, of course. But what happens in our families also impacts our *communities*. And what happens in our communities impacts larger *metropolitan areas.* And what happens in those larger metros impacts our *states,* which impacts whole *regions,* which impacts the *nation.*

Throughout history, America has benefited from this virtuous cycle founded on the family. Healthy families produced not just healthy children—not just healthy individuals—but entire generations of healthy families. Our nation has flourished because its families flourished.

Unfortunately, there's another side to that coin. If the ripple effect of healthy families creates blessings for a nation, that same effect will produce a curse when those families are unhealthy. Unhealthy families produce not just unhealthy individuals but entire generations of unhealthy families.

Which is exactly what we're seeing in our culture today.

American Families Are in Decline

When I was five or six years old, a burglar broke into our home. That experience of invasion is always distressing for a child, but more upsetting was the fact that the robber came through my bedroom window. At night. When I was fast asleep.

Thankfully, I stayed asleep throughout the robbery. (Even now, I hate to think what might have happened if I had awakened and tried to sound the alarm.) But the experience shook me profoundly when I found out about it the next morning. It scared me in a way I had never experienced before.

Of course, the big problem was that my dad wasn't in the picture at the time. He wasn't around, which meant it was just my mom and two little boys in the home. I've always known her to be tough, but her presence alone did not calm my fear.

The next night, and for many nights thereafter, I had a terrible time falling asleep. Whenever I started to drift toward unconsciousness,

I jerked back awake. Terrified. *What if someone comes through the window again? Should I yell? Should I try to fight? Should I run away?*

Mom tried to comfort me before bed and at different times through the night, but she was already exhausted. Eventually, the situation got bad enough that she purchased a gun for home protection. It was always stored safely away, and I almost never saw it, but knowing a means of defense was in the house helped calm my anxiety.

I share that story because it was one of the first times I recognized that something was deeply wrong with our family. I realized, in my childish way, that we were dealing with troubles, hazards, and worries that had no place in our lives. Something was broken that needed to be fixed.

In a similar way, I have come to understand in recent years that something is deeply wrong with American families in general. Something is broken that needs to be fixed.

I could spend whole volumes describing the various symptoms and problems currently plaguing families, and I'm sure you are all too aware of many major concerns as well. But let's focus on two specific ways in which American families are experiencing a notable decline.

A Decline in Quantity

First, American families are experiencing significant decline in terms of quantity. Meaning, a much lower percentage of Americans are enjoying the benefits of family—especially traditional families.

Let's start with marriage. In 1960, which was the height of the postwar baby boom, more than two-thirds of adults (67.4 percent, to be precise) were married.[5] A large majority of American adults experienced life through the lens of marriage. By the year 2000, only 54.4 percent of American adults were married.[6] By 2021, the portion of American adults living with a spouse dropped to 48 percent—less than half for the first time in our nation's history.[7]

Fewer people are getting married in our nation, which has resulted in fewer families in total—and, unfortunately, fewer traditional families.

In 1960, 73 percent of children in America lived with two married parents in their first marriage. Thus, just under three-quarters of children in the United States received the benefit of a traditional family. By 1980, only 61 percent of children lived in a traditional family. By that time, divorce was much more acceptable, which meant that many children were growing up in blended families. Many more were in single families, especially in situations where a single mother raised her children alone.

By 2015, less than half (46 percent) of all children in America were raised in traditional families, and that number continues to drop as the years go by.[8]

This is a crisis. Remember, we saw in chapter 1 that children raised in traditional families do much better in terms of overall health and success than children raised outside of traditional families. When they become adults, children from nuclear families experience more wealth, more education, and less crime than children from nonnuclear families. So, the more we see a decline in the quantity of traditional families, the more we will see a decline in the overall quality of life for future generations.

Just as importantly, the quantitative decline in the family is leading to a demographic crisis connected to birth rates in the United States. In 1950, there were twenty-four births for every thousand people living in America. In 1980, there were fifteen births for every thousand people. In 2023, we were down to twelve births per thousand. Meaning, half as many babies are born in America today as there were in 1950.[9]

There are many reasons for the declining birth rate in America. Abortion is certainly a major factor, given that more than 63 million pregnancies were terminated during the fifty years in which *Roe v. Wade* was the law of the land.[10] Birth control is another major factor, since pregnancy can now be decoupled from the act of sex. But the fact also remains that fewer people are getting married, and those who do marry typically tie the knot later in life than people in previous generations. Fewer marriages mean fewer children.

Why is this a problem? Economists have long tracked the "replacement level," which is the number of births needed to sustain a population. That replacement level is typically believed to be 2.1 births for every woman in a nation. The bad news is that the United States dipped below that birth rate back in the 1970s. The worse news is that our birth rate has continued to decline, as mentioned above. All of which means that our population will continue to trend older and older until we begin to experience the kind of unsustainable problems currently plaguing China and Japan.

Fewer children will mean a society that cannot sustain itself—one that will eventually collapse due to the strain of older generations needing to carry out the work of an economy with fewer young generations to replace them.

America is in the midst of that collapse. Indeed, the US population grew only 0.1 percent in 2021, which is the lowest level of growth since America was founded.[11] Certainly COVID-19 played a part in that low number, but the trends are moving in the wrong direction. If nothing is done, the population of our nation will soon cease to grow entirely—and begin to decline.

A Decline in Quality

When Candy and I first married, we spoke often about the excitement and anticipation of having children. We talked about baby names. We wondered whether our first child would be a boy or a girl. We imagined the wonder of all the "firsts" we would get to experience—first steps, first words, first time riding a bicycle, first day of school, and much more. As a young married couple, we were genuinely enthusiastic about the prospect of starting our family.

Yet we did not start our family. Not for several years. Why? Because

Candy and I married right after my second year of medical school. We knew the next two years of my education would be demanding in every way possible. The same would be true of my residency as someone who hoped to become a neurosurgeon. Today there is a limit of eighty to eighty-eight hours a week on the job for medical residents, but that wasn't the case back then. It was common for me to work more than one hundred hours in a given week during those early years.

So Candy and I waited to pursue the privilege of having children. We had a vision for the health of our home that was incompatible with a loving but absent father. In other words, we made decisions and set priorities because we valued the quality of our future family. Yet, sadly, the quality of family life in America today is impoverished and has been declining for decades.

This type of thinking about quality of family isn't prevalent today, as many Americans live their lives for the sole purpose of pursuing happiness and fulfilling their every desire.

In so many ways, families in America are broken. Something is wrong, and we need help. Take divorce, for example. Too many think of divorce as simply the end of a marriage. But that's not an accurate definition. Divorce is the tearing apart of a family. In fact, divorce is often the tearing apart of multiple families—even multiple generations of families, given that children whose parents divorce are more likely to choose divorce for themselves later in life.

Connected to the increase in divorce has been the rise of what experts call "multi-partner fertility"—parents who have children with more than one partner. It has become common in our culture for fathers to have children with several different women, and for mothers to have children with several different men. Sometimes the children of these multi-partner parents are gathered together in the same home, while in other situations they are scattered throughout different communities.

Now, am I saying that multi-partner families or blended households are less valuable than traditional families? By no means. All families are equally valuable because all families are made up of women, men, and children who carry the image of God.

At the same time, blended families and multi-partner parenting situations often face more complications than traditional families. By their nature, such families create obstacles and challenges that make it more difficult for both parents and children to succeed.

Another evidence of the qualitative decline in American families can be seen in the waning influence that parents have in their children's lives. It used to be that mothers and fathers were the primary sources of guidance for their children. Parents were the main vehicle through which children received their values, priorities, and worldview. This historical pattern is important for the internal health of families because parents know what's best for their children and are in the best position to provide for their children's needs.

In recent decades, however, this vital connection between parent and child has been threatened and eroded in several ways. Through entertainment media, social media, and an overzealous educational system, modern children are bombarded with content that produces real harm in their lives and pressures them to adopt values they do not understand.

Think about the never-ending stream of pornography pouring into homes via the internet, cell phones, smart TVs, game consoles, and other devices. Think about young children compelled to rehearse and regurgitate gender doctrines they cannot possibly understand—including being exposed to pornographic material in the should-be-safe confines of school libraries. Think about teens harmed by cyberbullying. Think about teens carrying the constant weight of comparison (and the constant reminder of their imperfections) as a result of social media values.

Even with the most vigilant and loving parents, it's hard to imagine how any children in our current culture could grow up unscathed by these destructive forces.

We can come up with many other examples that show how the quality of American families has declined in recent decades and is still declining today—child abuse, domestic violence, financial strain, the lack of appropriate housing, the rise in crime, the rise in addictions, the rise in diseases of despair, and much more. But again, you don't need me to call out each and every corrosive element at work against our families. You are already experiencing the consequences of the strain on American families—and so is America itself.

America Is Experiencing the Consequences

There's an old saw in politics that says elections—and especially presidential elections—always boil down to one main question for each voter: "Are you better off now than you were four years ago?"

More and more, the answer for Americans and American families is an emphatic no, regardless of which party is currently enjoying power on national, state, and local levels. More and more as I study what is becoming of America—both internally and in comparison with other nations around the world—I see a nation in decline.

It would be easy to write off the decline in American families as a symptom or result of the decline experienced by America itself. My goal in these pages is to show you that the decline of the American family is a *primary cause* of the decline we are witnessing in America. Individual families are not suffering because America at large has wandered from the promise and potential of its early days. No, America has been forced away from that promise and potential by means of the deterioration of American families, which have always served as a critical foundation for our nation.

We will explore *how* and *why* this has happened (and is still happening) in the middle chapters of this book. For now, let's take a deeper look at the consequences of this fundamental change. The weakening of American families has weakened our communities, our cultures, and our nation as a whole.

Communities in Crisis

One of the blessings of America is its diversity in the many types of communities established throughout the nation. You can live in a rural county, small town, suburb, or local neighborhood or borough of a major city and still be an American. The tragedy is that each of those different communities has experienced negative consequences because of the attack against American families in recent decades.

We don't have space to explore every example of those consequences, so I will focus on two of the most evident—education and crime.

During my early years as a child, I didn't do well at school. The struggles I experienced at home made it difficult to concentrate or apply myself well in the classroom, and I was wounded by my lack of success. Even the idea of going to school was depressing because I knew my teachers and peers would point out my inadequacies. Dealing with deep-seated doubts about my own capabilities, I decided to endure the classroom without really investing any effort.

There was just one problem with my plan—my mother. Sonya Carson was a tireless advocate for education, rightly understanding that school was the best and most profitable pathway out of poverty for my brother and me. Whenever I tried to get out of school, Mom let me know in no uncertain terms that I would be at my desk or be in big trouble. Whenever I failed a test, she held my feet to the fire. She did everything possible to lift up the value of education in our lives.

It worked. I eventually gained a better understanding of how to be a student, which allowed my natural talents to thrive and grow. I'm deeply grateful for my mother's persistent influence, and also for the American school system that maximized my efforts.

Unfortunately, that school system has not thrived in recent decades. Instead, it has degraded. Each year, the United States spends a staggering $14,891 per student in the public school system.[12] That is a tremendous amount of money to invest in our children, which is good. What is not good, however, is the diminishing returns we continue to see on that investment. According to the Programme for International Student Assessment (PISA), America ranks ninth among developed nations when it comes to students' overall scores in reading. We rank sixteenth in our science scores. And we rank thirty-fourth in math scores, falling behind such educational powerhouses as Estonia, Latvia, and Malta.[13]

It's important to remember that these national scores begin at the community level. For example, a recent investigative report from Project Baltimore states that 40 percent of Baltimore city high schools did not have a single student who scored "proficient" in math, based on standardized tests. Thirteen separate high schools did not produce a single student who achieved a basic proficiency at math for their grade level. Perhaps worse, of the 1,736 students who participated in those standardized tests, a full 74 percent completely failed their math assessment, scoring 1 out of a possible 4.[14]

This is not to pick on the city of Baltimore; many other school systems are performing at similarly low levels. My point is this: during the same time period in which traditional families have declined in America, local educational systems have suffered greatly.

Speaking of the classroom, would you believe I used to walk by myself to school when I was as young as first and second grade? Both in Detroit and Boston, I walked to school without fear. In Boston, I even used public transportation on my own and never questioned my safety. Similarly, I remember a time when Americans did not lock their doors at night—again, even in places such as Detroit and Boston.

Would such a thing be possible for young children in America's communities today? I highly doubt it. Our communities are no longer safe.

FBI statistics show that many types of crime have increased over the past decade, including violent crime.[15] But beyond the statistics, who among us hasn't been disgusted by videos of "mostly peaceful protests" erupting into chaotic scenes of buildings on fire, property vandalized, vehicles destroyed, and innocent bystanders attacked on the streets? Who hasn't seen videos of marauding gangs crowding into retail stores and stealing huge amounts of merchandise in broad daylight? Who hasn't been affected by story after story of women assaulted on college campuses and in all kinds of public venues?

I think it is safe to say that the combination of more crime and less safety is particularly devastating for families.

Cultures in Crisis

In the same way that America benefits from a diverse range of communities, there are many important subcultures that join together to form a larger American ethos. These subcultures are a critical part of everyday life in America, and they are also experiencing negative consequences because of the decline of traditional families.

For example, faith has always been a vital building block of American life. As a nation, America was founded on the belief that God is not only real but actively involved in human affairs. The Declaration of Independence famously begins with a national reliance on God's provision: "We hold these truths to be self-evident, that all men are created equal, that they are endowed by their Creator with certain unalienable Rights, that among these are Life, Liberty and the pursuit of Happiness."[16]

For most of America's history, faith has been a common denominator when determining morality—our accepted code of conduct in society and our cultural mores. Specifically, the Ten Commandments served as the bedrock for both our social expectations and our legal system.

However, America's reliance on faith is rapidly declining. Fewer Americans believe in God than ever before. Church attendance has been declining for decades. More and more, religious affiliation is seen as a liability rather than a benefit for a person's well-being and advancement. (We will take a deeper look in chapter 5 at America's erosion of faith, where I'll provide specific statistics.)

The result of our faltering faith is that America no longer has an agreed-upon system of morality. What one person thinks is right and good may seem abhorrent to another, and vice versa. We've lost our shared language of right and wrong. As a result, American culture (not to mention American families and individuals) is being torn apart by illicit drug use, sexual promiscuity and perversion, fiscal irresponsibility, selfishness, disrespect for others, hatred, moral relativism, lack of patriotism, decreased faith, increased secularism, decreased concern about the rights of others, and increasing authoritarianism.

Individual cities or regions often produce their own subculture within the broader scope of America. The lifestyles and attitudes of New Yorkers, for example, are often different from those in the rural South. Other regions such as New Orleans or Las Vegas or Miami have their own individual cultures built around particular styles of music, forms of entertainment, geographic specialties (such as beaches), and more.

What's interesting is that many specific cities and regions that have devalued, or even been antagonistic toward, traditional families in recent decades have experienced significant decline.

San Francisco is an interesting case study. With its intensively progressive views on sexuality, gender, and race, San Francisco has developed a reputation of being especially antagonistic toward traditional families. Part of this antagonism is values based, with the city demonstrating open hostility to individuals or families who oppose homosexuality or transgenderism, even on religious grounds. Another part of this antagonism is financial. As city leaders hoover up more and more tax money to pay for social welfare programs, many families have found it fiscally impossible to stay in the city.

After many years of this type of thinking and these kinds of policies, it's interesting to note how much San Francisco has deteriorated. According to the Hoover Institution, residents of San Francisco have a one in sixteen chance each year of being the victim of a property crime or violent crime. That means San Francisco is more dangerous than 98 percent of cities in America, whether those cities are large or small.[17]

Property crimes in particular have skyrocketed—so much so that many residents have taken to leaving the trunks of their cars open when parking in the downtown area. Why? So that would-be thieves don't break their car windows when searching for plunder.

The situation is so bad that many retail businesses have closed what should be profitable stores in the city, including Starbucks, Walgreens, AT&T, Banana Republic, Target, Nordstrom, and more. The mall operator Westfield gave up control of an entire mall due to what it called "challenging operating conditions," which include crime, homelessness, rampant drug use, and high taxes.[18] Things have degraded so much and so quickly that a quarter of a million residents have fled San Francisco since 2020, seeking greener pastures elsewhere.[19]

In many ways, San Francisco (and to a degree California as a whole) has become a microcosm of my principal argument for this chapter—namely, that attacks against the family in a community or nation will result in drastically negative consequences for that community or nation. When the family is in decline—especially traditional families—cultures will suffer.

A Nation in Crisis

Finally, the assault against traditional families in America has resulted in numerous negative consequences for the United States as a whole. We've already seen the way America has declined in relation to other countries in important categories such as education, healthcare, and overall quality of life. So let's focus on two specific symptoms of America's decline—symptoms I believe are specifically tied to the deterioration of traditional families.

The first symptom is the huge rise in what doctors call "diseases of despair," which include such maladies as anxiety, depression, addiction, and suicidality. You may have seen surprising statistics connected to these diseases in recent years, including:

- One out of every twenty people was diagnosed with a substance abuse issue or suicidal tendencies during the years between 2009 and 2018.[20]
- The rate of those diagnoses increased by 68 percent during that time span.[21]
- More than one out of every six adults (18 percent) are dealing with depression, which is a jump of 7 percent from 2015.[22]
- Anxiety rates have risen from 5 percent in 2008 to almost 7 percent of American adults in 2018.[23]

In short, America is wallowing in despair and desperation, and things are only getting worse. Importantly, most of these data points were captured before the COVID-19 pandemic, which has certainly caused further increases in these maladies and other diseases of despair.

Why do I think these increases are connected with the decline of traditional families in our nation? For at least a couple of reasons. The first is medical. Healthy adults should not suffer from anxiety, depression, addiction, or suicide—at least not in most cases. Yes, there can be chemical imbalances and other factors that cause real problems in otherwise healthy people, but those instances should be the exception, not the rule.

The rise in diseases of despair shows that something is wrong or out of tune with the fabric of our society. And because these increases coincide with the decline in both the quantity and quality of family life, I feel this connection is too strong to ignore.

The other reason I believe diseases of despair are connected to the erosion of the family is the demographics of the data. Studies have consistently shown that diseases of despair are skyrocketing among younger generations—especially in the areas of addiction, anxiety, and suicidality. This is critical, in my opinion, because younger generations are less likely to be raised in traditional families. Many people in those younger generations lack stability and support in their family lives, and they are suffering as a result.

The second symptom of America's broader decline is the rapid rise of *polarization* among its citizens. Put simply, people are becoming more and more extreme. This symptom is clearly evident in the political realm, where voters have increasingly become more polarized across recent decades. But it's also true in other arenas, such as morality, social issues, and even entertainment options such as in the sports world.

More and more people operate with an "us versus them" mentality. We see the world in terms of "our side" (we are always correct) and "their side" (they are always wrong). We believe that in order for our side to win, the other side must actively lose, which means we have a difficult time finding common ground or seeking compromise.

This is a troubling state. Even thirty or forty years ago, people could be solidly Republican or solidly Democrat and still see the virtues of those on the other side. Individuals from both political parties could still function well as friends and family members. But this is less and less the case today.

Many have rightly pointed out that cable news and social media algorithms play a huge role in widening the divide in the American populace. But that truth ignores a larger question: Why are modern people so easily influenced by outside factors and outside opinions? Why are we so easily pushed further toward the extreme?

A major part of the answer to those questions, in my opinion, is that so many adults today did not receive traditional values as they grew up and matured. Many of today's adults had their worldviews formed by television shows or peer pressure rather than the specific, intentional transfer of priorities from parent to child. As a result, we remain easily influenced by extremists who are more than eager to tell us how to think and what to believe.

And yes, that's bad news. Indeed, we have covered many types of bad news within this chapter. The decline of American families, especially traditional families, has caused America as a whole to suffer loss. We are experiencing the consequences of abandoning the family as a key foundation for our communities, our cultures, and our nation.

There is good news though. It's not too late. We can still turn things around if we choose to engage in this perilous fight and strive once more for the good of all families.

THREE

The
AMERICAN FAMILY

Sometime after my father left the picture, my mother moved our young family to Boston for a couple years. She, myself, and my older brother, Curtis, took up residence in a typical tenement apartment with her brother-in-law and his family.

Uncle William worked in a meat-packing plant, which was certainly an advantageous situation for young and growing meat eaters like Curtis and me. He spent long hours at the factory, taking both regular shifts and overtime hours each week to keep a roof over our heads—his children and my mother's children. His sons were much older than Curtis and me, but we enjoyed them immensely.

I can still remember sitting very still and quiet in Uncle William's kitchen, which also doubled as his makeshift barbershop, as he told us about life as he worked. His words of wisdom mingled smoothly with the buzz of the clippers, the smell of shaving cream, and the sudden shock of a hot towel on cold skin.

Uncle William bought me my first car. When I graduated from Yale University, he drove to New Haven, Connecticut, with my mother and my Aunt Jean. After the ceremony, he presented me with a five-year-old Pontiac LeMans that broke down on a weekly basis. I must say, I learned a lot about car engines from that wonderful gift!

I'll never forget the look on Uncle William's face when he gave me the keys. The pride I saw there. The joy. Likewise, I'll never forget the moment several years later when I presented Uncle William with his own set of keys. By then I had experienced great success as a neurosurgeon, and I noticed the way Uncle William admired the almost-new Lincoln Continental I recently purchased. I handed him the keys, and I felt that same pride settle over my own features. That same joy.

It's true that I experienced many struggles during my developmental years. Life without a father was difficult. Living as two families in a Boston tenement built for one family did not provide much room for privacy or personal space. Watching my mom drag herself back and forth between three jobs every week was painful—especially because I knew she maintained her grueling schedule to secure not her future, but my own.

So yes, I have witnessed the stress and strain of family life in circumstances that were less than ideal. But I have also witnessed moments of gladness. And wonder. And peace.

I have seen the power of American families—as a child, as a father, and now as a grandfather. I have seen the power to produce good in a world that is so often desperate for goodness. And gladness. And wonder. And peace.

This has been true throughout the life of our nation—and it can be true again if we are willing to stand up and support such a critical institution.

America Is Exceptional

There has been a lot of debate over the years about the idea of American exceptionalism. Is America the same as most other wealthy nations around the world—just a bit larger in terms of geography and a bit younger on the national stage—or is there something about America that makes it truly unique? I am in favor of the latter view. I see America as unique in history and still unique in today's world.

One of the greatest evidences of that uniqueness is the fact that millions of people attempt to become part of American society every year.

Much has been made of the immigration crisis at our southern border—a crisis greatly exacerbated during the Biden administration. What many don't realize, however, is that it's not only immigrants from Mexico seeking to enter the United States. In recent years, US border agents have encountered immigrants, refugees, and asylum seekers from more than one hundred different countries.

Much of the world views America with such high esteem that people are willing to spend all they have and endure significant hardship just to seek a chance at building a life within our borders.

So, what is it about America that has earned such a reputation? What is it that makes America unique?

One answer is our history—more specifically, the unique circumstances that led to America's founding as a nation. Those who traveled to the "new world" both before and after the signing of the Declaration of Independence did so because they understood the tremendous value of freedom. Reaching America from other parts of the world was not easy, which means America was founded by brave and hardy souls willing to risk hardship in order to reap the reward of opportunity.

Importantly, those early settlers and citizens also placed a high value on worship, and specifically the freedom to worship as they pleased. The majority of America's earliest citizens were Christians, and our nation as a whole was built on the foundation of Judeo-Christian values—on loving God and loving our neighbor.

Yet in the broad scope of American history, the freedom to worship has attracted millions of others from faith traditions outside of Christianity. In fact, America has been a place where every type of religion and religious expression can flourish and has flourished. Why? Because America has protected religious freedom in all forms.

We must continue to do so in order for that critically important value to continue to thrive.

Furthermore, self-reliance and self-improvement through hard work are two additional values that have been critical during the development of America's culture. These are the foundational elements of the American Dream, which is the idea that every citizen in this nation has the opportunity to elevate themselves and build a legacy if they are willing to put in the effort.

I've never met anyone who was a bigger advocate for those values than my own mother. Sonya Carson absolutely detested the practice of blaming others or making excuses for our problems. In fact, whenever I or my brother started to make excuses for falling short of her standard in one area or another, she would recite this poem written by Mayme White Miller:

> If things go bad for you—
> And make you a bit ashamed,
> Often you will find out that
> You have yourself to blame . . .
>
> Swiftly we ran to mischief
> And then the bad luck came.
> Why do we fault others?
> We have ourselves to blame . . .
>
> Whatever happens to us,
> Here are the words we say,
> "Had it not been for so-and-so
> Things wouldn't have gone that way."
>
> And if you are short of friends,
> I'll tell you what to do—
> Make an examination,
> You'll find the fault's in you . . .

You're the captain of your ship,

So agree with the same—

If you travel downward,

You have yourself to blame.[1]

My mother would be ashamed of the victim mentality that has gripped many younger people in America today—especially those in the Black community who pin all of their problems on slavery or racism. Of course, those ideas were around during my younger years, but my mother was a vigilant gardener who prevented them from taking root in our lives. She made me read *Up from Slavery* by Booker T. Washington, which taught me the value of self-sufficiency. She helped me find biographies of inventors, which taught me there are always new and better ways to do things. She brought me books by entrepreneurs, which taught me how to achieve my goals. She helped me read about scientists, explorers, and doctors, which helped me realize I had to be committed to intense study and hard work if I wanted to achieve my loftiest goals. These values are part of what has always made America great, and they must be defended.

What other values have been instrumental in American culture? Grit, determination, and courage come to mind. Those characteristics were vital in our victories at war—especially the great and terrible conflicts we know as World War I and World War II.

America's leaders in particular have demonstrated courage through their ability to see the big picture and make hard decisions. I think of President Kennedy defying Nikita Khrushchev during the Cuban missile crisis. Kennedy understood that a failure to act in the moment would lead to a much bigger crisis in the future, and so he refused to be bullied, even by the threat of nuclear annihilation.

That kind of courage is lacking in many of our modern leaders. Sadly, the grit and determination of our past have been swapped for apathy and appeasement in the present. These are poor substitutes.

Finally, one of the most intriguing aspects of American culture (and American exceptionalism) is our great diversity. As I've said, the nation we call America is a conglomeration of people from a multitude of other nations. We are a people joined together from around the world, which gives us tremendous advantages because we can share and learn from many different points of view. American culture has long been a combination of the very best from a broad range of cultures. This is true for entertainment, industries and businesses, education, religious expression, and more.

Importantly, the value of diversity will remain positive and constructive for only as long as we can maintain unity as a nation. For much of our history, America was strong because the diverse elements of our population had values in common and a shared pride in the promise of America.

It's no secret that this unity has begun to crumble in recent decades, and more especially in recent years. Accord has given way to squabbling, and the implications for our nation are dire.

America Is Exceptional Because of Its Families

Why am I interested in exploring these exceptional elements of American culture? Because they are deeply connected to American families.

Certainly, American families have benefited from our nation's history, faith, opportunity for self-improvement, determination, courage, and diversity. Those qualities are fertile soil in which all types of families can grow and thrive. Yet in another example of a virtuous circle, American families have been the major roots or foundations of those cultural benefits. In many ways it is because of American families that America itself has been so exceptional.

Let's look at this virtuous cycle in terms of three specific categories.

1. Families Fostered America's Faith

If you walked into just about any home during the eighteenth or nineteenth centuries in America, chances are quite good you would have seen the following displayed prominently on a wall within that home:

1. Thou shalt have no other gods before me.
2. Thou shalt not make unto thee any graven image.
3. Thou shalt not take the name of the LORD thy God in vain.
4. Remember the sabbath day, to keep it holy.
5. Honor thy father and thy mother.
6. Thou shalt not kill.
7. Thou shalt not commit adultery.
8. Thou shalt not steal.
9. Thou shalt not bear false witness against thy neighbor.
10. Thou shalt not covet.[2]

It didn't matter what type of home you entered—a rural farmhouse, a city apartment, a sharecropper's shack, all the way up to the grandest of mansions. The Ten Commandments would be there.

Of course, those Ten Commandments did not originate in families. They were given to us by God through His Word. Yet, importantly, those commandments were primarily disseminated and enforced through the vehicle of families—in those days, traditional families. It was mothers who cross-stitched those commandments into visible form and hung them on the walls. It was parents who had their children recite those teachings at breakfast or dinner (or both). And it was fathers who enforced the household penalty for breaking one of those commandments.

The result, as mentioned earlier, was a common language of morality within our nation. The rules and expectations were written down for all to see. They were talked about. They were memorized and recited. And when those rules were broken within a family, it was more than likely to be the family that doled out the consequences.

This system was in place for many facets of faith. Families talked about God together. They prayed together. They worshiped together. As a result, they matured together. They learned how to think respectfully of others, take personal responsibility, and seek out their place within God's plan for the nation.

Thus, families thrived and communities thrived. Along the way, our nation thrived. A virtuous cycle.

2. Families Fostered America's Prosperity

In the same way families played a primary role in developing and disseminating America's strong sense of faith, those families also served as a major source of America's prosperity. Of course, most families did not generate significant income within the home, but those homes certainly cultivated the characteristics that were necessary for our nation's success.

Think about the virtue of hard work, for example. That virtue was not learned in school, even when public schools became a common part of American life. Students then were the same as students now in that the expectations of a school system *reveal* the character of young people rather than *produce* that character. Books, radio programs, and, later, television shows may have reinforced the value of hard work, but they did not provide opportunities to practice that value.

Rather, families instilled the expectation that parents work hard to provide for their children, and that children work hard to learn and grow and contribute not only to the household but also to the community. Families provided genuine opportunities for hard work that resulted in genuine benefits.

The same is true when it comes to many other ingredients that have been necessary for America's prosperity—ingenuity, innovation, creativity, determination, perseverance, vision, and more. Those characteristics were essential to the growth of America's corporations, but they did not originate in those corporations; they originated through families in which individuals were allowed to grow, mature, and discover their giftings— and not only discover them, but maximize them through the blessing of love and support.

From its earliest stages, people understood that America was a land of opportunity—a place where any person could seek and achieve advancement through hard work and determination. But families were the vehicles through which that opportunity became reality. For example, individuals blazed trails throughout the West, but it was families that joined together to populate those territories and establish thriving communities. Politicians expanded the borders of American territory, but families made those borders practical by being fruitful and multiplying in every conceivable way.

Similarly, the American family has played a major role in the ability of Americans not only to maintain wealth and prosperity throughout their lifetimes, but to multiply that prosperity from generation to generation.

I recently spent time with several Vietnamese families who came to America forty years ago as boat people. They were virtually penniless when they arrived, but that first generation put their heads down and worked hard. They put in long hours to secure a home, and they made the education of their children a top priority. Over time, that family experienced enormous success. In fact, I met them at a large speaking event, and I was fascinated to learn that they were major sponsors.

During our conversation, I shared something I have often noticed about immigrant families. "The first generation starts by sweeping floors at a gas station," I said. "Then the next time I'm there, those who were sweeping are now pumping gas. Then they're behind the cash register. Then they own the whole station."

My Vietnamese friends laughed and nodded their heads before I even finished my observation. They knew exactly what I was talking about, and they carried a deep appreciation for all the ways their families had been able to thrive from decade to decade and generation to generation in our nation.

In the same way, our nation has thrived because of families that take advantage of their opportunities to flourish. In doing so, they bless their local communities, their cities, and finally the country as a whole.

Another virtuous cycle.

3. Families Still Foster the American Spirit

I have talked about previous generations of American life because I want to show that families were critical to the formation of America's culture from the very beginning. But it's also true that families foster the same American spirit that continues to make our nation exceptional in our world.

For several years, I've had the privilege of working with a young man named Andrew Hughes. He was my chief of staff at Housing and Urban Development, and he has stayed with me as executive director and CEO of the American Cornerstone Institute.

In my earliest associations with Andrew, I knew he and his wife, Kara, had desired children for many years. After much prayer and with the aid of medical technology, they finally achieved the pregnancy they desired for so long. All of us were overjoyed as the baby developed and approached its entrance into the world.

Then one day, I received a call from Andrew at an unusual hour. I was traveling for HUD at the time, but as soon as I heard his voice, I knew something was terribly wrong. Fighting back tears, Andrew informed me that their daughter had been diagnosed in utero with what neurologists call a vein of Galen malformation—a very rare but serious vascular malformation in the brain that is often fatal. This particular lesion was very complex and sadly was not amenable to surgery or any other form of intervention.

"Doc" (his nickname for me), "they're saying she's not going to make it."

Andrew and Kara named their little girl Harper, and they prayed for her fervently for weeks. I joined them, as did many others. Even so, within a few hours of Harper's birth, she passed away. Andrew and Kara were blessed to hold their daughter and shower her with love for the entirety of her short life.

I've known many young couples who would have fallen apart after such a tragedy. In fact, I am familiar with many marriages that did fall apart after the death of a child. Thankfully, Andrew and Kara are both the products of strong families and are therefore themselves strong as individuals. They were able to support each other and receive support from those who love them, and they made it through.

Today, Andrew and Kara are closer than ever. The Hughes family has been blessed with three young and healthy children—Hope and Henry, who are twins, and young Reagan.

During their time in the hospital, Andrew's pastor shared with him the story in the Bible of the time David lost a child only a few days after he was born. God promised David that he would bear another son, who turned out to be Solomon—the man famous for his wisdom. Solomon also happens to be my middle name, and I was pleased to learn that little Henry Hughes was given Solomon as his middle name both to honor me and the memory of his older sister.

The reason I share that story is to show that the virtuous cycle connecting American families with America itself still exists. My friend Andrew is a young man who serves not only his own family but the entire nation. Indeed, Andrew was the youngest and longest-serving chief of staff in the entire Trump administration.

There are many other iterations of the Hughes family still growing and thriving throughout America today—still prospering and contributing to the prosperity of others. This virtuous cycle that helped build America is still spinning, yet there is danger on the horizon.

America Is in Danger

There are few constants in human history, but one of them seems to be the fact that civilizations are cyclical. They rise, flourish, and fall. Sometimes the rising and flourishing is rapid, while other times sustained success is built more slowly. Sometimes the collapse happens seemingly in a single moment, while other times the fall drags out over decades, or even centuries. But the relentless reality of empires seems to be their temporary nature. What goes up must come down.

Think of the greatness of ancient Egypt, Babylon, or the Mayan empire. Think of the continual swapping out of dynasties throughout the vast history of China. Think of Alexander the Great weeping because he had no more worlds to conquer. In more recent years, think of the seeming invincibility of the Russian Federation and the crumbling of the Berlin Wall.

Many scientists have studied the trajectory of these civilizations. Most notable is *The History of the Decline and Fall of the Roman Empire* by Edward Gibbon. It's interesting that similarities and patterns emerge as we dig into the history of great empires and world powers.

I recently came across the research of Alexander Tyler, who was a professor at the University of Edinburgh near the end of the eighteenth century. Tyler took a special interest in the rise and fall of democratic civilizations, and he posited eight specific stages that can be observed in those types of nations throughout history. (While there seems to be some question about the historical accuracy of attributing these stages to Tyler, I find them useful as a thought exercise.)

Here are the eight stages:

1. **From bondage to spiritual growth.** Most civilizations are formed in the crucible of difficult times. For example, many of the earliest settlers in America came to these shores in an effort

to escape persecution. Even in the original thirteen colonies, religious persecution existed, as the Puritans (who were a majority) demanded that others follow their religious standards. The more freedom took root, however, the easier it was for citizens to experience genuine spiritual growth.

2. **From spiritual growth to great courage.** Having had their character forged through difficult times, courageous leaders emerge who are willing to sacrifice personally and inspire others to do the same in order to achieve a common good. It still amazes me, for example, that a ragtag continental army was able to prevail against the most powerful military empire on the planet.

3. **From great courage to liberty.** Having thrown off oppression, a new civilization takes root on the foundation of key ideals. Heroism and freedom are esteemed and celebrated. In America, an ideal of liberty and justice for all was quickly established and became the envy of the world.

4. **From liberty to abundance.** Freedom almost always results in prosperity for those who enjoy it. Yet one of the dangers of that prosperity is abundance—or overabundance. Prosperity in America resulted in the development of a middle class in a size and scale that is unique in human history.

5. **From abundance to complacency.** It's a sad fact of human nature that overabundance more often than not leads to overindulgence. When a nation has plenty of resources, it is prone to ignore problems that signal danger ahead. America experienced great abundance during the twentieth century, yet the existence of two world wars and the Cold War allowed its citizens to remain vigilant. That vigilance has waned in recent decades, however.

6. **From complacency to apathy.** Prolonged periods of complacency seem to be the death knell of democratic civilizations, as people become more and more dismissive of real problems.

Especially corrosive is the lack of care for our own neighbors within a community. In America, recent decades have seen this kind of apathy toward the struggles of others, and our current experience is filled with Americans who directly attack or prey on others in their communities.

7. **From apathy to dependence.** Apathetic people lose the virtues of hard work, passion, and self-reliance. As a result, they respond positively when others offer to take care of them. This is especially true in democracies where people begin to vote en masse for whichever politicians make the biggest promises, regardless of whether those promises are actually kept.

8. **From dependence back to bondage.** The more people look for others to take care of them, the more power centralizes. Dependent people become desperate, looking for strong central leadership to solve their problems, which opens the door for dictators or more powerful nations or groups to seize control.

Sadly, America now seems to be moving toward the latter stages of this cycle. Complacency and apathy are commonplace. And while the idea of "relying on others to take care of me" was once antithetical to the American ideal, more and more people actively desire a "big government" that promises to solve all of their problems by reaching deeper and deeper into their lives.

What's more, while America remains the dominant superpower in our modern world, its dominance is currently being threatened by China. What many people don't understand is that China as a nation—and especially the Chinese Communist Party, which is the centralized government—has very different values and operates with very different priorities than those that define American culture. Chinese culture is based on a centralized, authoritarian form of government that limits freedom and promotes conformity. Such a style of governing would have been unthinkable in the United States even two decades ago, but as we'll see later, things are changing.

America is changing.

What hope is there for a return to courage, liberty, and abundance? Much hope! Even now, I strongly believe in the promise and the power of America. Yet if our nation is going to course-correct and return to the greatness of its past, it will need to do so through the vehicle of American families.

That reality makes it especially critical for us to recognize the truth that American families are under attack.

FOUR

ENEMIES
at the GATES
(*and*) INSIDE)

It's hard to imagine a more horrifying day for a nation than what Israel experienced on October 7, 2023. That particular Saturday was a Sabbath, of course, and a major Jewish holiday known as Simchat Torah—typically one of the happiest days of the year.

Around 6:30 in the morning, the terrorist organization known as Hamas used drones to disable many of the cell towers along Israel's border with Gaza, which made it difficult for military officials to monitor video cameras stationed along the border wall. Other drones destroyed automated machine guns installed along the border to discourage incursions.

Hamas then launched thousands of rockets from inside the Gaza Strip, all aimed at different targets throughout Israel. About the same time, terrorist leaders used earthmoving equipment to knock down large segments of the border wall between Israel and Gaza, which allowed hundreds of terrorist soldiers to pour into Israel. Other terrorists used paragliders to fly above the border wall in separate areas.

The next several hours were horrifying in every sense of the word. More than 1,500 Hamas fighters overwhelmed four military posts stationed near the border. Many Israeli soldiers were killed in their sleep, including unit commanders. Several were taken captive and dragged back into Gaza. Few escaped.

Unchecked, the terrorists continued their assault by ravaging several towns near the border. They murdered civilians indiscriminately, slaughtering women and children—even babies. They butchered the residents of a kibbutz. They descended in rage upon a large music festival, killing and raping and dragging more hostages back to their hidden warrens and secret tunnels inside Gaza City.

All told, more than 1,200 Israelis were murdered in less than a day. More than 240 were abducted as hostages and forced to endure brutal treatment. Many of those hostages were later killed.[1]

The events of October 7, 2023, in Israel have been linked to September 11, 2001, in America. That is certainly a natural connection, but it doesn't go far enough from Israel's perspective. Given the vast difference in population, what happened to Israel would be akin to forty thousand Americans dying in the September 11 attacks rather than three thousand—not to mention the capture of more than three thousand hostages by the same terrorists who executed the attack.

No matter how you look at it, October 7 was a dark day not just for Israel but for our world.

The question is: How did it happen? How did a group of terrorists score a victory against the best-armed, best-trained, and most-advanced military in the Middle East?

The answer seems to be *coordination*. None of Hamas's attacks on that day were new—the drones, the rockets, the paragliders, the bulldozers, the individual soldiers seeking to steal, kill, and destroy. All of those tactics had been used before, and Israel was aware of them. What was new, however, was the coordination of those attacks at a single time and in a specific order that was carefully calculated to overwhelm Israel's defenses.

A similar attack is taking place against America, specifically against American families. As we'll see here, and in the chapters to come, the enemies of America are waging a prolonged, coordinated, multipronged assault with the specific goal of devastating our families.

In this chapter, I want to look at three big questions connected to this attack—who, how, and why.

Who Is Leading the Attack?

To put it plainly, the enemies of American families are the enemies of America itself.

Remember, American families have always been a key foundation for America's health and prosperity. It is especially true of traditional families. Remember also that economists and sociologists have long been aware of the benefits of traditional families. Individuals who grow up in families where married parents raise their own children experience more prosperity, less poverty, and less crime than those raised in nontraditional settings.

For these reasons and more, what we know as the traditional family has long been a primary target for those who seek the downfall of the United States.

Who, then, is leading the assault in this perilous fight? Who are the enemies of America who seek to weaken America by weakening its families?

The first answer is Marxists, or what we might call socialists today. Many may scoff at that idea, largely because Communism, Marxism, and socialism have performed so poorly in the past century. Those of us who lived through the Cold War may have an especially difficult time believing that socialism would remain a threat, given all the evidence against it.

That evidence includes these important facts:

+ Many scholars theorize that Communist and socialist leaders were directly responsible for more than 100 million deaths throughout the twentieth century. That includes the Communist regimes of Joseph Stalin in Russia, as well as regimes in Eastern Europe, China, Cuba, North Korea, Vietnam, and Cambodia.[2]
+ Of the many countries liberated by the collapse of the Soviet Union, none of those countries elected to rebuild their nations using a

socialist model. They saw firsthand the devastation brought about as a result of that model.

- In the modern world, there are only five nations that are decidedly "Communist": China, Cuba, Laos, North Korea, and Vietnam. None of those nations can match the United States in terms of military strength, economic prosperity, and longevity.

In so many ways, the socialist wave of the twentieth century remains the greatest catastrophe in human history. You may wonder, then, *How could such an ineffective wave actually be a threat to American families, let alone to America itself?*

Good question. The answer is both simple and frightening.

During the height of Communist influence and power in the middle of the twentieth century, plans were put in place for a socialist takeover of the United States. This takeover would not be accomplished by military might or economic power. In fact, this takeover was not planned as a "takeover," per se, in which an outside force would dominate America into accepting a socialist way of life. Instead, this takeover was designed to occur from within.

Back in 1958, a former FBI agent named W. Cleon Skousen wrote a book called *The Naked Communist*. Based on years of investigation, the book was a detailed record of the Communist movement in the 1900s and of Communist goals during Skousen's day. Specifically, he highlighted forty-five "current Communist goals"—plans that were being set in motion for the ideological capture of America.

Some of those goals are shocking when we read them today. For example:

- "Promote the U.N. as the only hope for mankind. If its charter is rewritten, demand that it be set up as a one-world government with its own independent forces."

- "Capture one or both of the political parties in the United States."
- "Use technical decisions of the courts to weaken basic American institutions by claiming their activities violate civil rights."
- "Get control of the schools. Use them as transmission belts for socialism and current Communist propaganda. Soften the curriculum. Get control of teachers' associations. Put the party line in textbooks."
- "Gain control of all student newspapers."
- "Infiltrate the press. Get control of book-review assignments, editorial writing, policy-making positions."
- "Gain control of key positions in radio, TV, and motion pictures."
- "Continue discrediting American culture by degrading all forms of artistic expression. An American Communist cell was told to 'eliminate all good sculpture from parks and buildings, substitute shapeless, awkward, and meaningless forms.')"
- "Break down cultural standards of morality by promoting pornography and obscenity in books, magazines, motion pictures, radio, and TV."
- "Infiltrate the churches and replace revealed religion with 'social' religion. Discredit the Bible and emphasize the need for intellectual maturity which does not need a 'religious crutch.'"
- "Eliminate prayer or any phase of religious expression in the schools on the ground that it violates the principle of 'separation of church and state.'"
- "Discredit the family as an institution. Encourage promiscuity and easy divorce."
- "Emphasize the need to raise children away from the negative influence of parents. Attribute prejudices, mental blocks, and retarding of children to suppressive influence of parents."[3]

If you find it difficult to believe those words were written in 1958, I sympathize. There is no denying that they were. I encourage you to purchase your own copy of *The Naked Communist* and read these words for yourself. The entire book is quite helpful in laying out much of the playbook currently being used by progressives, socialists, and others who seek to replace America's original vision and values with something much, much different.

In fact, *The Naked Communist* was so explosive in the years after its original publication that large portions of it were read into the Congressional Record on January 10, 1963.[4]

Clearly, one of the main goals of socialist advocates at the height of their influence was to destabilize the key foundations of American society, with the eventual goal of destabilizing (and then destroying) America itself. As we've already seen in these pages, the traditional family has been and still is a major foundation for America's prosperity and the overall wellness of American citizens.

Thus, the traditional family has been and currently remains under attack. We will continue to explore several avenues for that attack in the pages that follow.

Besides Marxists and socialists, globalists are another category of the "enemies at the gate" who are seeking to weaken American families. Globalists are those who desire a one-world economy and a one-world system of government.

For centuries, leaders and empires have desired to "conquer the world"—Alexander the Great, Genghis Khan, Napoleon, the Ottoman Empire, the Roman Empire, even the British Empire. For the vast majority of human history, however, such a goal has been unrealistic in practice. The distances were far too slow in terms of communication and far too large in terms of maintaining a physical threat capable of commanding obedience.

Only in the past century or so has technology advanced to such a point that a unified, global system of government could be feasible. The same is true for a unified, global economy based on a single currency. It is no coincidence, then, that the concept of globalism, or "globalization" as it is sometimes called, has gained much ground during that time, and especially in recent decades.

You can see globalism at work through the relatively recent creation of worldwide institutions designed to bind all nations together. The United Nations was the first of such institutions, of course, and it remains quite influential. Sadly, it also remains quite ineffective at doing anything productive, such as lifting people out of poverty or dissuading terrorist states from actively investing in terrorism, but that is another topic for another place.

Other examples of globalist institutions include the World Trade Organization, the International Monetary Fund, the World Bank, the World Health Organization, the International Development Association, the World Economic Forum, and more. The recent rise in regular multinational summits—such as the G20 and the G8 gatherings—follow a similar emphasis on globalism. And of course, the presence of huge multinational companies such as Alphabet (Google), Meta (Facebook), Amazon, Apple, and many others have also "flattened" the globe, to use Thomas Friedman's term.[5]

It's important to note that I am not claiming that these organizations are nefarious in and of themselves, or that they are actively seeking the downfall of America. Rather, they are all examples of the relatively modern push to bind together as many nations as possible in as many ways as possible.

What I do believe, and what seems obvious based on common sense, is that globalization cannot abide the presence of global superpowers. The exceptional nature of America has made it an exception to many of the goals and strategies pursued by much of the rest of the world. Therefore, it is reasonable to conclude that those who desire a global government also desire a weakened America that will better fit into that unified structure.

And as we've seen, the weakening of the traditional family in America continues to be the primary method for weakening America itself and whittling away at America's exceptionalism.

How Is the Attack Being Carried Out?

We are wading deeper into the troubled waters of what I call our perilous fight—the long-planned attempt by America's enemies to systematically erode what has made this country exceptional and then change our nation into something fundamentally different from what it has been. This fight involves huge forces working at the highest levels of society, all grinding away at the promise of our United States.

Such concepts are scary to think about, I know. What is even scarier—and even more tragic—is that American families have become the primary target of these forces.

That raises the question, how are the attacks against America and American families being carried out? We saw some of the most threatening goals of America's enemies listed above, but what methods are being used to accomplish those goals? Where are the battlefields?

We will highlight several specific answers to those questions in the chapters to come. Right now, however, let's explore some of the general methods being used to coordinate this widespread assault against the family.

First, the assault against America and its families has been carried out for decades through the educational system, which includes both public education and higher education. Remember these statements from *The Naked Communist*? "Get control of the schools. Use them as transition belts for socialism and Communist propaganda. Soften the curriculum. Get control of teachers' associations. Put the party line in textbooks."

It's hard to understate the degree to which these goals have been accomplished over the past fifty years.

I remember many times during my early years as a father when I heard about this teacher or that teacher making radical claims in the classroom. We'd hear whispers about teachers or administrators holding extreme views of one kind or another. For the most part, I ignored these whispers. I knew many of my sons' teachers and found them to be wonderful people. Certainly, it became known that teachers as a whole seemed to "lean left," especially as the years went by. But I was not alarmed—not yet.

Many people felt the same way. For several decades leading into the 1990s, it was generally assumed that schools were healthy places that had the best interests of students in mind. Sadly, in recent years, those assumptions have been dispelled in several shocking ways.

For example, social media has played a major role in revealing specific methods used by teachers to indoctrinate their students with radical ideologies including socialism, racial hatred, gender confusion, and even straight-up pornography—not all teachers, of course, but we find so many examples that it may sometimes feel that way.

I think of Chaya Raichik as someone on the front lines of exposing these methods. Chaya began posting an anonymous Twitter (now X) handle called "LibsofTikTok" to poke fun at the often hysterical and hypocritical videos of those advocating a progressive agenda. At first, the goal was simply to be humorous. But the more Chaya began to dig into the world of progressive thinkers—and especially into the videos of progressive teachers—the more appalled she became.

Raichik began to post videos of teachers bragging about indoctrinating their students, which has helped open the eyes of many viewers. Many of the teachers Raichik exposed were fired after their antics became public. After being doxed by the *Washington Post*, which revealed her name publicly for the first time, Raichik continued the work of a good investigative journalist by exposing the ways children's hospitals actively push vulnerable young people toward the transgender movement and permanent, life-altering surgeries.

Through the work of Chaya Raichik and others like her, many people have come to understand the role that teachers unions play in the indoctrination of children rather than the education of children, which is their sole responsibility. An investigation during the 2022 midterm elections revealed that teachers unions had donated millions of dollars to political campaigns, with the vast majority of that money distributed to progressive candidates.[6]

When it comes to higher education, it has been an open secret for decades that the majority of college professors have a liberal bent, which makes them sympathetic to socialism and often downright antagonistic toward America's capitalism.

Back in 1989, right when the Soviet Union was crumbling because of failed Communist practices, the *New York Times* ran an article titled "The Mainstreaming of Marxism in U.S. Colleges." The article described the irony of the moment: Communism failed spectacularly and tragically in the real-world setting of the Soviet Bloc, and yet the philosophies of Marxism and socialism thrived in the world of academia.

Here's how Felicity Barringer began her article: "As Karl Marx's ideological heirs in Communist nations struggle to transform his political legacy, his intellectual heirs on American campuses have virtually completed their own transformation from brash, beleaguered outsiders to assimilated academic insiders."[7]

For more than thirty years now, those same college professors have enjoyed free reign to saturate their students with Marxist views. For more than thirty years, generations of college graduates have carried those ideals into American culture and important American institutions—media, government, the arts, businesses, human resources departments, and, of course, schools. Many of those early graduates have become teachers and professors themselves, which means the cycle continues to spiral upward—or downward, depending on your point of view. This slow, sustained effort at ideological capture is what many Communists refer to as "the long march through the institutions."[8]

As noted in *The Naked Communist*, this long march has also targeted the Democrat political party with much success. In 2010, about 55 percent of Democrats had a positive view of socialism, according to Gallup. In 2021, that number had risen to 65 percent. More Democrats felt positively about socialism than about capitalism.[9] This helps explain the rise of outspoken socialist politicians such as Bernie Sanders and Alexandria Ocasio-Cortez.

As a reminder, the philosophy of Marxism has always targeted the family as an enemy that must be destroyed, or at least marginalized. Karl Marx called for "Abolition [*Aufhebung*] of the family" in his *Communist Manifesto*, writing that what we know as the traditional family was nothing more than a false institution based on maintaining capital from generation to generation.[10] Therefore, the rise in Marxist (socialist) thinking naturally corresponds to the rising assault on traditional families in America.

Another way that assault has been carried out is through our entertainment media. We can see this assault in two ways.

The first is the continual portrayal of traditional families as outdated or laughable in movies, TV shows, books, podcasts, and other forms of artistic expression. It was, of course, common in my day for traditional families to be lifted up in movies and TV shows as examples worthy of emulation. Parents were depicted as wise caregivers who desired the best for their children. Yes, they made mistakes, but those mistakes were resolved in ways that drew the family closer together.

Think of shows such as *Little House on the Prairie*, *The Waltons*, *The Andy Griffith Show*, *Family Ties*, *Family Matters*, and even *The Fresh Prince of Bel-Air*.

Sadly, beginning in the '90s and accelerating to the present, Hollywood has largely abandoned traditional families as cornerstones of movies and TV shows. Instead, they feature "modern families" in which the father is often an idiot, the mother is frazzled but wise, and the children are often obnoxious snobs. Most of these families are blended or feature single parents. Many actively promote homosexuality or transgenderism as normal, healthy lifestyles that should be celebrated more than the old-fashioned families where Mom and Dad raise their own children and work through issues together.

The second way entertainment media has carried out its assault against the family is much more dangerous. We see it in the sharp rise of obscenity pumped into homes in recent decades. The assault begins with the so-called "soft porn" viewable by children and adults through modern movies and TV shows, as well as through social media. It seems rare for Hollywood to produce anything these days that does not include sex scenes or barely dressed characters, not to mention the glorification of violence, drugs, and other harmful behaviors.

But "soft" almost inevitably leads to "hard." A recent report revealed that 73 percent of teens regularly watch pornography online. More than 15 percent of those teens were first exposed to pornography at age ten *or younger*.[11]

What's critical to understand about our culture is that these figures are intentional! Obscenity is not trickling into people's lives by accident; it is being pumped into our homes for specific purposes. To wit, 58 percent of teens were exposed to pornography without looking for it, and 63 percent of those who were exposed without looking for it reported that they had been exposed only *in the past week*.[12]

Our families are under direct assault.

Finally, a third answer to the "how" question has to do with the press, or corporate media. The Founding Fathers wisely added "freedom of the press" as a core component of the First Amendment. In a healthy society, a free press is needed to disseminate information to the people in ways they can understand, and to do so in a way that is free from bias and free from direct regulation by the state. The press should be a critical tool for speaking truth.

Sadly, our mainstream media has fallen well short of that standard, both today and throughout previous decades. Instead of sharing information with the public, modern media has become quite adept at hiding information from the public when that information doesn't match the narrative they want to convey. And rather than speaking truth to power, modern media actively seeks to serve those in power who agree with their ideologies and to attack those who do not.

More and more, the mainstream media within America has become a tool for accelerating the weakening of America. This is clearly evident, for example, in the way media personalities regularly and consistently stoke racial hatred in our country.

How many times have you seen headlines similar to the following?

- "A White Man Fatally Shoots 3 Black People at a Florida Store in a Hate Crime, Then Kills Himself."[13]
- "Prosecutor: White Woman Who Killed Black Neighbor amid Ongoing Feud Won't Face Murder Charge."[14]
- "'I'm Drowning': Black Teen Cried for Help as White Teen Tried to Kill Him, Police Say."[15]

Each of the headlines above is from an actual news story covered by the mainstream media. It seems like we hear stories like that all the time.

Yet how often have you seen headlines like these?

- "Black Teen Murders Three Black Teens in Chicago."
- "A Crowd of Mostly Black Women and Men Rob Another Walmart on the South Side of San Francisco."
- "Latino Man Murders White Girlfriend and Her White Children."

Would you expect to see such headlines on a mainstream website or the chyron of a nightly news channel? Of course not. It goes without saying that all crimes should be reported, regardless of race. But our media consistently emphasizes crimes that match the first list and ignores those that match the second list.

These and other reasons help explain why only 32 percent of Americans have a "great deal" of trust in the mainstream media, while 68 percent have "not very much" trust or "none at all."[16]

Even so, the media still demonstrates a huge amount of control over the information and ideas that become part of the conversation in our culture. And much of what the media chooses to present is actively harmful to families, especially traditional families. That includes:

+ consciously eroding or deriding the importance of faith in America as a whole and in families in particular.
+ continually pushing the narrative that divorce is healthy and necessary and doesn't really have much impact on the lives of children.
+ continually pushing the narrative that mothers must have a career in order to be fulfilled, and that such a career will have no impact on a mother's relationship with her children.
+ continually pushing the narrative that fathers are unnecessary, or that involvement in the lives of their children is an "added benefit" rather than a necessity.
+ continually pushing the narrative that homosexuality is a natural and even preferable alternative to traditional families, which is harmful because an increase in homosexual relationships will logically lead to a decrease in children and to a decrease in families.
+ seeking to drive a wedge between parents and children in terms of transgender ideologies, as in portraying parents as villains for expressing skepticism toward young children who believe they were born as the wrong gender.
+ seeking to drive a wedge between parents and children when it comes to questions of authority, such as school choice or COVID-19 vaccines.

You may have noticed a common denominator in the three groups mentioned above—the movers and shakers of the educational system, the entertainment media, and the press. All three of those groups are now dominated by the "elite" of American culture—those who have advanced college educations, large incomes, positions of prestige, or a combination of those qualities.

It has become quite fashionable among the elite of our society to demonize capitalism as an inherently evil system—even though that system has benefited them to a great degree—and to lift up socialism as a morally superior alternative. Some of these individuals genuinely believe they are helping the downtrodden by peddling in Marxist thinking; some are simply virtue signaling—hoping they will be seen as caring for those less fortunate.

In this way, the elite of America often function as "useful idiots"—a term used by Vladimir Lenin to describe the gullible believers who sympathize with socialist ideals and therefore undertake, without realizing it, to bring about the end of their own privileged positions, an end that may well include the weakening or eventual destruction of America.

Why Attack the Family?

We've seen *who* is driving the assault against American families. The primary culprits are modern-day Marxists and globalists who wish to destabilize or outright destroy America and weaken its place on the world stage. They are attacking American families, especially the traditional family, because they understand that families have always served as a key foundation of America's strength and prosperity.

We've also explored some aspects of *how* this assault has been and is being carried out. Those who wish to see America fall have been playing a long game of institutional capture and control. They have specifically targeted our nation's educational system, entertainment media, and corporate press as vital tools for hollowing out America from within.

Let's close this chapter by looking at another important factor as to *why* the family has become such an important battleground for this assault—namely, that weakening our families results in weakened individuals who are easier to bully and control.

I'd like you to imagine an individual who was raised in a strong family. This person grew up with their mother and father for their childhood and teen years, and they are secure in the knowledge that their parents love them. Their parents have proven their love over and over again through emotional support, financial support, and through the imparting of the kinds of values and skills necessary for success in life.

That same individual is also a person of faith. They grew up going to church and learning about the Bible. At some point, often during the teen years, this individual experienced a personal encounter with the Creator of the universe. They stopped learning *about* God and started enjoying a relationship *with* God. This person knows what they believe and values that faith more than just about anything else.

Finally, imagine this individual was raised in America and has a great respect for their nation of origin. They understand the freedoms they are granted in America—freedoms that are not present in many other nations. They also understand the opportunity they have to grow up in the United States, and that if they work hard, receive an education, and get married before having children, the odds are that they'll be able to lead a successful life.

In summary, this person is supported by a three-legged stool of family, faith, and country.

Do you know such a person in real life—someone in your circle of friends, your family members, or perhaps your classmates or coworkers? Are you even such a person yourself?

If so, then you understand the power and confidence typically produced by such a strong foundation. Such people are anchored to solid ground, which means they are able to stand firm when the winds of trouble blow. It's hard to push them around, bully them, or control them. It's not that such people are perfect or never make mistakes—certainly they do. But they are equipped with the kind of maturity and mental vigor that helps them continue moving toward success even when the path is difficult.

Conversely, it is known among psychologists and experts in other fields that those who fail to develop strong familial bonds often struggle as adults. Those with *secure* attachment styles generally have a positive view of themselves and positive interactions with others. Those with *anxious, avoidant,* or *fearful* attachment styles—which typically occur when we don't feel secure in our relationship with our mother, father, or both parents—view themselves more negatively and have greater difficulty forming healthy relationships as adults.

Here's my point: Those who are attempting to steer America toward socialist or globalist directions desire a strong centralized government that reaches into every area of our lives as private citizens. They desire the government to control our finances, education, emotional health, physical health, sexuality, and even spirituality.

That control becomes extremely difficult when America is populated by tens of millions of individuals who are confident in themselves and protective of their freedoms, which is a natural outcome of being raised in strong families.

Therefore, traditional families are under attack. Those who want to weaken America are actively attempting to weaken traditional families so that America will be filled with individuals who are not only compliant about government control but who actively desire government control because they are dependent on the state.

This is why we must actively take up such a perilous fight—not only for our nation, but also for our families and our own health and wellness as individual citizens. In the following chapters, we will explore some of the major battlegrounds involved in that fight.

FIVE

ERODING *the* FOUNDATIONS *of* FAITH

It was May 24, 2020, when Mike McClure decided he'd had enough.

As senior pastor of Calvary Chapel in San Jose, California, McClure became more and more frustrated by Santa Clara County rules regarding COVID-19. A "shelter in place" order was still in effect, requiring residents to remain at home unless participating in essential activities. All churches and houses of worship were closed down, including Calvary Chapel.

As a pastor, McClure knew his people were suffering. He heard story after story of congregants feeling lonely and filled with despair in their isolation. People were desperate for some sense of normalcy in a world turned upside down.

So Pastor McClure made his decision: the church would reopen and weekend gatherings would recommence. McClure went so far as to declare that his church would never shut its doors again.

True to his word, Calvary Chapel relaunched its worship services at the end of May and never looked back. The services were packed. They included public singing—which had been banned by the county—and involved many participants who chose not to wear masks—which were still required by both the county and California as a whole.

That's when the backlash began.

In a state already known for seeking to control its residents, Santa Clara County created policies that were particularly insidious. For example, county residents were urged to snitch on individuals or organizations out of compliance with regulations. A special website and hotline were set up to receive these anonymous reports.

Journalist David Zweig reported on what happened next:

> On August 21, 2020, in response to one such complaint, Calvary was
> served with a cease-and-desist letter for holding indoor gatherings, for
> failing to ensure everyone wore masks, for failing to ensure social dis-
> tancing, and for failure to ensure there was no singing. Two days later,
> enforcement officers arrived at the church and reported observing at least
> 100 unmasked people gathered inside, not distancing, and with some of
> them singing.[1]

In the following weeks and months, the county's health department
and "business compliance unit" continued stealthy surveillance and public
reprimands. County officials set up dozens of stakeouts, including video
surveillance, at a neighboring church within view of Calvary's campus.
Those same officials watched livestream video of the church's worship
services to seek out masking and social-distancing violators. When the
county granted a restraining order to business compliance officers, they
entered the church building during a worship service. They even recorded
worshipers sharing sensitive prayer requests.

The most outlandish (and outrageous) tactic was the county's use
of digital surveillance against the church. Officials spent a large amount
of money to access cell phone data from an aggregation company called
SafeGraph, which tracks data (including location information) from 47
million mobile devices across the United States. Then those same officials
spent more money to hire a Stanford law professor to analyze the data and
determine how many people were entering Calvary Chapel on a given day.

In the end, Santa Clara County leveled more than $2.7 million in
fines against Calvary Chapel for violating its COVID-19 restrictions.
Importantly, those same restrictions allowed most shopping malls, retail
stores, and even museums to remain open during the same period for
which Calvary received its fines.[2]

Zweig's article garnered a lot of attention when it was published, given the over-the-top nature of Santa Clara's onslaught against a house of worship. Even progressive-leaning political commentator Nate Silver was shocked, noting, "It's kind of crazy (and tells you a lot about who was writing the restrictions) that churches in some jurisdictions were subject to more restrictions than museums! Not even attempting to follow any sort of epidemiological principles."[3]

Of course, in hindsight, we know our government overreacted and overstepped its bounds in many ways during the COVID-19 years. Many of the rules and restrictions imposed during those years made no sense at the time—closing beaches, shutting down small businesses and forcing everyone to gather at big-box stores, and compelling the wearing of masks outdoors. Other restrictions have been confirmed as silly as we look back now, such as closing schools and mandating cloth masks in indoor spaces.

What I found especially interesting about the COVID-19 pandemic, however, was the way those extraordinary circumstances revealed "the man behind the curtain" when it comes to our government's active desire to establish control in the lives of private citizens. During those years, we saw more clearly than ever the extreme methods used by governments to manipulate citizens. Sadly, this took place even in America.

One of the truths revealed during those COVID-19 years—and one I found especially shocking and disturbing—is how eagerly certain members of our government want to curtail religious freedom in this nation, including the freedom to worship. Those efforts are not new, as we'll see below. But they are increasing at a rapid pace.

The reason I am dedicating a chapter of this book to that topic is that faith and family are deeply connected. Even as families are a critical foundation for our nation, faith—the freedom to worship our Creator—is the foundation of all families. I say that because families are a gift from God as revealed in His Word.

Therefore, the efforts to erode the foundations of faith in America have caused great harm to families and will continue to do so until those efforts are thwarted.

The Value of Faith

In these pages, I've already referred to several of the ways faith in God has been both a foundation and a foundational blessing of America. Most of our Founding Fathers were people of faith, and they had no qualms about referencing that faith in the founding documents, including the Constitution and the Declaration of Independence.

In fact, it's clear the founders believed in the moral necessity of their actions *because of* their faith in God, not in spite of that faith. Their faith spurred them to reject tyranny and create a nation where people could be free: "We hold these truths to be self-evident, that all men are created equal, that they are endowed by their Creator with certain unalienable rights, that among these are Life, Liberty and the pursuit of Happiness."[4]

Many people point to "the separation of church and state" as evidence that belief in God should be minimized or even discouraged. They often cite the Constitution as the source of that principle—or, more accurately, they infer that principle from the Constitution. But that is backward thinking, plain and simple, once we understand the context of that document.

Most of the original thirteen American colonies had formalized religious preferences. The majority were affiliated with Protestant denominations, while others were Catholic. In those years before America became its own nation, it was common for colonial officials to persecute and punish those from other denominations who attempted to proselytize. For example, if Catholics came into a Protestant colony and started to promote Catholicism, they often faced serious consequences. The same would be true for atheists or members of other religions.

It was for that reason that Thomas Jefferson and the other founders sought to protect religious freedom in the Constitution—even the freedom to reject religion. The Bill of Rights declares, "Congress shall make no law respecting an establishment of religion."[5]

The goal was always to protect religious freedom, making sure the government did not maintain adherence to one religious expression over another. That freedom to worship has been a core element of America's success from the very beginning.

It has certainly been a core element in my own success. I've mentioned some of the more painful aspects of my childhood, most notably the absence of my father and our family's struggle with poverty. But there were many wonderful elements of my childhood as well—largely because of my mother.

Sonya Carson was a woman of great faith, and she took great pains to make Christ the center of our home. She recited Bible stories to us from the time we were small children. She made sure we attended church faithfully every week—actually, several times a week. I still remember the way we opened and closed each Sabbath with prayer, singing, and playing musical instruments.

As I matured, I developed a faith of my own—one that was not dependent on my mother's beliefs. Following in her footsteps, I developed the discipline of praying about virtually everything. I prayed about school. I prayed for my friends. I prayed about sports. I spent quite a lot of time praying that my mother and father would get back together.

In terms of my personality, I used to have a very quick and sharp temper. I had a habit of internally erupting in explosive anger at even the slightest provocation. I kept these eruptions hidden from most people because I wanted to be seen as an upstanding young man, but my anger did break out against my family members and closest friends. As a young teen, I felt the conviction of God in my heart about this tendency. I realized my anger was an offshoot of my self-centeredness. The more I focused on myself and all the ways my wants and wishes were unmet, the more my rage boiled inside me. Only with God's help was I able to move the focus off of myself and let go of that anger. In doing so, I let go of my temper as well.

My relationship with God became especially important when my brother graduated from high school and left for college. All of a sudden, I was alone most of the time, which could have easily opened the door for mischief. Thankfully, my desire to honor God steered me toward more productive pursuits, such as visiting libraries and museums.

I remember settling down onto my knees in prayer as I prepared for my own transition to college. I only had enough money to apply to one university because in those days an application fee was required. After a great deal of prayer, I decided to apply to Yale. Clinging to the promise of Proverbs 10:24, I sent in the application: "The fear of the wicked will come upon him, and the desire of the righteous will be granted."

I was accepted, and I felt anew the abiding joy of knowing I was not on my own in this life. My heavenly Father was on my side.

Many years later when I took my position at HUD, I anticipated great enthusiasm from my colleagues for bringing a God-centered worldview back to that agency. After all, HUD had largely taken over the work of faith-based organizations in providing housing and other societal necessities for the downtrodden members of our society. I assumed, perhaps naively, that those who managed our nation's efforts to serve the poor and needy would likewise be motivated by faith. That assumption proved incorrect on many occasions. In fact, it wasn't long after I started serving at HUD that a senior administration official admonished me to "cut out the God stuff."

Sadly, such an attitude has become all too common in today's progressively secular society. The constitutional blessing we know as freedom *of* religion has been twisted and reinterpreted to be freedom *from* religion. As a result, many who are antagonistic toward religion believe they have a government-approved license to attack policies, programs, organizations, and even individuals amenable to faith.

In other words, faith is under attack. Faith as a foundation of American culture is eroding. Tragically, this erosion is happening both from without and within.

Faith Is under Attack from the Outside

In 1958, a man named Edward Lewis Schempp filed a lawsuit on behalf of his family against the school district of Abingdon Township in Pennsylvania. At that time, it was mandatory in Pennsylvania for public schools to begin each day with a reading from the Bible. Schempp, his wife, and his two children were Unitarians; they claimed these readings violated their constitutional rights and interfered with the free exercise of their religious faith. The lawsuit also targeted the school's practice of having students recite the Lord's Prayer at the beginning of each day.

The school district made several attempts to accommodate the Schempps. So did the state of Pennsylvania, which amended its law and allowed parents to exempt their children from the daily Bible readings and prayer if they desired. The Schempps were not appeased, and the lawsuit proceeded forward.

By 1963, the case had made its way to the Supreme Court. In a majority opinion of 8–1, the Court ruled in favor of the Schempp family, declaring that mandatory prayer and Bible reading in public schools were unconstitutional. But that's not all. The Court went several steps further in directly attacking religious freedom in our nation.

Specifically, the Supreme Court endorsed the view that the Establishment Clause—the section of the Bill of Right that states,

"Congress shall make no law respecting an establishment of religion"—was not meant merely to prevent the government from favoring one religion over another. Instead, the Court ruled that the government may not promote any specific form of religion, or even religion in general.

In taking this extraneous and harmful step, the Court used the dissenting opinion from an earlier case in which a single justice wrote, "The [First] Amendment's purpose was not to strike merely at the official establishment of a single sect, creed or religion . . . [but] to create a complete and permanent separation of the spheres of religious activity and civil authority by comprehensively forbidding every form of public aid or support for religion."[6]

Of course, such an assertion was silly. It makes no sense to claim the founders intended a "complete and permanent separation" between government and faith when those same founders utilized religious claims and ideals as the foundation of that government in the very documents that declared their independence!

Still, that was the direction taken by the Court. And it is that Supreme Court decision, rather than the Constitution itself, from which our modern legal system has adopted the notion of "the separation of church and state."

I find it difficult to overstate what a watershed moment that court decision was in American history. From that point forward, faith and religious freedom have been under active assault in our nation. Not only was mandatory prayer removed from schools, but many people have used that ruling to declare that no form of prayer is allowed in schools. The same is true for the reading of Scripture and the displaying of the Ten Commandments.

Think for a moment about that last point. For centuries, the Ten Commandments served as common ground for what is acceptable and unacceptable in society. A moral code that everyone could understand—and did understand, even if they chose to violate that code.

Look at these commandments for yourself:

1. Thou shalt have no other gods before me.
2. Thou shalt not make unto thee any graven image.
3. Thou shalt not take the name of the Lord thy God in vain.
4. Remember the Sabbath day, to keep it holy.
5. Honor thy father and thy mother.
6. Thou shalt not kill.
7. Thou shalt not commit adultery.
8. Thou shalt not steal.
9. Thou shalt not bear false witness.
10. Thou shalt not covet.[7]

Have schools become healthier in the past sixty years after these basic principles were removed? Are students safer? Are teachers better able to teach?

No. In fact, a recent survey from the National Education Association revealed that a staggering 55 percent of educators are considering leaving the classroom earlier than they planned, largely because of safety issues and the disrespect they receive from students.[8]

In recent years, you've likely seen many other examples of faith and religious freedom under attack from outside forces. Take, for instance, the story of Jack Philips, who owns the Masterpiece Cakeshop in Colorado. Philips underwent a long and brutal legal battle when he refused to make a wedding cake for a homosexual couple. His reasoning was that Scripture prohibits the practice of homosexuality—which is, in my view, a correct interpretation. Therefore, Philips was bound by his religious convictions not to produce a cake that celebrated those practices.

On the surface, it seems silly that any business owner or artist in America would be forced to produce something that violates their religious principles—especially in the context of a cake, given the dozens of bakeries to choose from in Denver. Still, Philips endured years of public abuse because of his decision, including mistreatment from the media.

The ensuing lawsuit went all the way to the Supreme Court, and Jack Philips won. The Court ruled that Colorado's state law could not force him to violate his religious convictions.[9] Yet on the exact day the Supreme Court decided to hear Mr. Philips's case, an attorney named Autumn Scardina contacted the Masterpiece Cakeshop and asked Philips to create a cake in celebration of Scardina's gender transition from male to female.[10]

That case is now heading to the Supreme Court. For a decade now, Jack Philips has been harassed because he chose to stand up for his religious beliefs—and that harassment is still continuing.

Another example of religious freedom under fire was exposed in 2023 when social media got wind of an internal FBI memo that specifically targeted Catholic citizens for extra scrutiny and surveillance. The title of the memo itself seems crazy: "Interest of Racially or Ethnically Motivated Violent Extremists in Radical-Traditionalist Catholic Ideology Almost Certainly Presents New Mitigation Opportunities." But the leaked memo was available for anyone to read.

In essence, the memo attempted to connect "radical traditionalists"—an oxymoron if I've ever heard one—in the Catholic church with White supremacists prone to physical violence.[11]

That memo was never intended to see the light of day. It was one of the numerous back-and-forth documents produced by the Justice Department, yet it revealed an active, intentional attempt to target and harass American citizens specifically because of their religious beliefs. Who knows what else is being communicated or what actions are being coordinated in the thousands of memos that remain secret?

There are many other examples—many of which I'm sure you are familiar with. But the overall takeaway is that religious freedom is under attack in America. Faith is under attack, sometimes even by the government itself. This attack has undoubtedly harmed families in our great nation, and undoubtedly will continue to do so unless we stand up and demand the religious protections guaranteed by our Founding Fathers.

Faith Is under Attack from the Inside

From a statistical perspective, the erosion of faith in America is impossible to deny. In 1972, 90 percent of adults in the United States identified as Christians, while 5 percent identified as "religious nones"—they had no religious affiliation. Fifty years later, only 63 percent of adults identify as Christians, while 29 percent identify as "religious nones."[12]

In 1970, a little more than 70 percent of American adults were members of a church, synagogue, or mosque. Today, only 47 percent are members. It was the year 2021 when the switch officially occurred—for the first time ever, the majority of adults in the United States were not church members.[13]

As we've seen, much of the overall decline in the number of Americans pursuing a relationship with God can be attributed to attempts from outside sources to discourage this pursuit. This interference is especially true when it comes to church attendance and other "public" aspects of faith that are now viewed by many as antiquated or even harmful.

Yet it cannot be denied that many internal factors have also contributed to the erosion of America's faith. Just as attacks from without have accelerated that erosion, so have attacks from within.

For example, hypocrisy is often cited by many who reject a belief in God. They point to Christians or members of other religions whose actions fail to match their words or beliefs. In the famous words of Brennan Manning, "The greatest single cause of atheism in the world today is Christians who acknowledge Jesus with their lips, walk out the door, and deny Him by their lifestyle. That is what an unbelieving world simply finds unbelievable."[14] These can be hard words to read, but they ring true. And they remind us of our important role as ambassadors for God's kingdom as we sojourn in this nation.

But individual hypocrisy is not the only obstacle to the health of the church. The church itself has declined in many ways throughout America. Not every denomination, and certainly not every individual house of worship. But enough churches have lost their way to make a noticeable difference in the overall quality of faith in our nation.

I think the history of my alma mater is a helpful picture for exploring the problems currently affecting the American church. As you may know, Yale University was originally founded as a divinity school. It was a college of religious training for Congregationalist ministers in Connecticut. Yale was also fiercely patriotic in its early days. In fact, it was Yale president Ezra Stiles who first saw the British fleet approaching New Haven, Connecticut, as he watched from the telescope in the steeple of the college chapel. The Yale student militia helped defend the town the following day.[15]

Over time, however, the leaders of Yale became interested in expanding beyond their roots of faith. Yale became a prestigious college—the largest and most respected in the new nation called America. As a result, the college brought in other types of professors with other types of interests. Theological studies went from a primary focus to one of many focuses—then, eventually, to a lesser focus.

In recent decades, many Yale professors and university administrators have become leading figures in the progressive movement—just as many were leaders of the socialist movement in America during the middle of the twentieth century. As a result, an institution originally founded with a primary mission to serve God and support people of faith is now openly antagonistic to those goals.

Sadly, many elements of the American church are in the throes of a similar progression. The mission and mandate of the church is clear:

And Jesus came and spoke to them, saying, "All authority has been given to Me in heaven and on earth. Go therefore and make disciples of all the nations, baptizing them in the name of the Father and of the Son and of the Holy Spirit, teaching them to observe all things that I have commanded you; and lo, I am with you always, even to the end of the age." (Matthew 28:18–20)

Spreading the gospel. Making disciples. Teaching the world about God's Word. These have always been the cornerstones of church ministry.

Yet over the centuries in America, other priorities have crept in and crowded out those noble goals. One of those priorities is money. As America has grown in prosperity, so too have its churches. Many churches have placed too much emphasis on budgetary goals and building projects rather than on fulfilling the Great Commission.

Some pastors and church leaders have overemphasized what is often called the "social gospel." Many churches, then, have become primarily humanitarian enterprises seeking to alleviate the suffering of the world without beating people over the head with the gospel. Obviously, the call to care for those in need is a vital part of the church's mission. But we go astray when we make these humanitarian efforts the *primary* mission of the church.

One reason focusing on social issues can become tricky is because our cultural views on social issues change frequently—and often radically— and yet Scripture does not change. Truth does not change.

Just fifty years ago, for example, our culture was firm in the belief that God is real and should be worshiped, that homosexuality is a sinful practice that should be avoided, and that gender always has been and always will be confined to a simple binary of male and female. Those were the majority views in American culture by huge margins. It also happened that those views aligned with the truth contained in the Bible.

Now, of course, our culture's views on those issues have shifted radically.

Unfortunately, many of our religious leaders have chosen to follow what culture believes rather than anchor themselves to what Scripture says is true.

And this shift points to a final way that faith in America has been eroded from within—namely, the fact that many religious leaders and institutions value cultural relevancy more than they value carrying out the Great Commission. Many denominations have chosen to make compromises rather than make disciples. Many religious leaders prefer to stand with the crowd rather than stand on Scripture. This is why we have churches encouraging no-fault divorce, blessing homosexual weddings, and ordaining pastors and bishops whose lives openly defy the message of God's Word.

One technical term for this phenomenon is "mission drift." Many churches and faith organizations have allowed tertiary priorities to become the main drivers of their ideas and actions, which has resulted in huge swathes of faith communities losing their way. The blind are leading the blind.

I know this is a difficult truth to swallow, and even a frightening reality to accept. But I'd like to end with a story I hope will offer some inspiration.

In my first year at Yale University, I had a particularly bad experience in my chemistry class. As a high schooler, I had developed a poor habit of slacking off during the semester and then studying very hard at the end to achieve high scores on midterms and finals. That strategy carried me through even my most difficult classes as a junior and senior, but it was not working well for me as a college freshman.

As my freshman year drew to a close, I knew I was in serious danger of flunking my chemistry class. In fact, things were so bad that I poured out my heart to God in prayer, asking what He wanted me to do with my life. I had always planned on a career in medicine, but failing chemistry would surely sink my chances of getting into medical school. So, I asked God for guidance on other directions I should pursue.

As it turns out, my chemistry teacher was either very magnanimous or very sadistic. He had a policy that any student failing the class could get double credit on the final exam. If I scored well on that exam, I could not only avoid failing but might actually achieve a good grade. Of course, I jumped at the chance.

The night before the exam, I decided I would stay up and read the entire chemistry textbook from front to back—all 800 pages. Obviously, that was a stupid plan, but I was naive. Less than an hour after I started reading, I fell fast asleep.

During that sleep, however, I had a vivid dream. I was alone in the chemistry lecture hall. I saw a somewhat nebulous figure appear and begin working out chemistry problems on the blackboard at the front of the hall. I watched, entranced, for what seemed like an hour. When I woke up in my dorm room early the next morning, I still remembered every detail of the dream. In fact, I was able to look up each of the problems the figure had solved in my textbook.

Somewhat bewildered, I made my way to class. When I opened the test booklet for the final exam, I was stunned to discover that the first problem on the test matched the first problem from my dream. The same was true for the second—and the third and the fourth, all the way to the end.

In short, I aced the test! I passed chemistry with a solid B, and I made a firm resolution to become a much more diligent student—a promise I kept as I finished Yale and progressed through medical school with distinction.

I tell that story because I learned a secret in my chemistry class that sustained me through all my years at Yale: God was there. God was with me.

By that time, Yale as a university had drifted far away from its initial founding as a divinity school for training pastors. It was a thoroughly secular institution and, in many ways, antagonistic toward the realm of faith.

Yet even in those halls, God was present, and He possesses the power to change lives.

It's true that many facets of the church have drifted away from God's plan and God's truth. There are even aspects of the church that seem to exist and operate in direct contradiction to His will as expressed in Scripture. Yet even so, God is here. God is still present in the church, and He is still mighty to save. He is still fully able to restore faith as a primary foundation, not only of our nation, but of our families.

Therefore, don't be discouraged. Don't give up hope. Instead, choose all the more to follow Jesus and join Him in this perilous fight.

SIX

ASSAULTING IDENTITY

For several years, Chrissy Teigen was one of the most popular and powerful celebrities in America. She was a model, a businesswoman, an author, and a celebrated cook. She also had a huge following on social media. In fact, back when Twitter was still called Twitter, many referred to her as the unofficial mayor of that platform.

It seems clear that Teigen delighted in her role as a cultural icon and a vocal leader among progressives. She posted her thoughts regularly and viciously, often seeming to relish tearing down those with whom she disagreed. Donald Trump was a favorite target, both before and during his presidency. Teigen also targeted many other people who expressed conservative views.

Teigen was especially influential in the practice of "canceling" other people, both on social media and in real life. While *canceling* is a nebulous term, it typically refers to a collective outpouring of abuse and threats against someone who has done something or said something deemed to be unorthodox, with the goal of humiliating that person into silence. Being canceled can also include seeking to get people fired from their jobs or removed from other professional ventures as punishment for "wrongthink."

In those instances when someone was getting canceled during Teigen's reign of terror, she was likely perched atop the bandwagon. In fact, Teigen played a role in the cancelation of food writer Alison Roman. It started in 2020 when Roman criticized Teigen for "selling out." Teigen publicly declared her hurt feelings, and the mob attacked. It didn't stop attacking until Roman was fired from her food column for the *New York Times* and canned from a cooking show.[1]

Then the bandwagon broke down—at least for Teigen. In May 2021, several people commented about how Teigen bullied a sixteen-year-old woman several years earlier. The person in question gained a measure of notoriety for marrying her acting coach, who was a much older man, and many people mocked her online—often cruelly.

But Teigen was especially vicious. "I hate you," she wrote to the teen. She sent multiple direct messages expressing her desire that the woman die, and she posted that same sentiment publicly: "My Friday fantasy: you. dirt nap. mmm baby."[2]

The backlash was immediate and intense. Teigen lost business deals and followers. She was branded as a bully and a purveyor of hate. She became a punch line for late-night television hosts. The public, it seemed, was gleeful at the thought of someone who had presided over the cancelations of others now being canceled herself.

There's a word commonly used in today's world to describe situations where cancel-ers become cancel-ees. That word is *woke*.

If you're shaking your head right now, I understand. For many of us, wokeness (or being woke) conjures images on a wide spectrum, with *silly* on one end and *frightening* on the other.

We might think of college students who put themselves above criticism even as they complain about the microaggressions they believe they are forced to endure. We might think of hypocritical young adults gathering to protest the evils of capitalism while sipping Starbucks and stomping their expensive shoes. Or we might think of middle-aged White women and men shouting down a Black conservative who, to their way of thinking, doesn't understand the evils of institutional racism.

All of these and more are illustrative elements of this new mosaic of thinking we call wokeness. It can be silly, insincere, and oxymoronic. But it can also be very dangerous.

In truth, woke is not a joke. Woke thinking—and especially woke policies—are causing significant harm to our nation and to our nation's families.

I want us to explore this detriment with a serious eye throughout this chapter. Specifically, I'd like to unpack the way wokeness and woke thinking assault our very identities as human beings—the way it erodes our understanding of even the most obvious assertions about who we are and what we are called to do. As we'll see, this assault has a profound impact on the crucial bonds we form in our families.

Wokeness Defined

Let's get on the same page by answering this question: What is wokeness?

Interestingly, to be "woke" started out as a positive term, implying that a woke person is someone who is socially conscious and aware. Rather than the masses who are asleep to the evils of prejudice and class warfare that are causing damage in our nation, many individuals declared themselves to be "awake" to those issues—or "woke." In the early days of the term's usage, to be woke was akin to being cool.

Wokeness is now typically viewed as a synonym for "stupidity." But finding a solid definition for wokeness seems especially difficult to pin down.

Conservative author and commentator Ben Shapiro has defined wokeness as the belief that "America is fundamentally racist, and that western civilization is, at root, similarly racist."[3] Liberal comedian and commentator Bill Maher has sought to make a separation between his brand of old-school liberalism and the new way of thinking we call wokeness. In similar fashion to Shapiro, Maher sees wokeness as a hyperfocus on race and racism—an emphasis that has gone from helpful to harmful. "Five, 10 years ago, bedrock liberalism was [that] we are striving to be a color blind society where we don't see race," he said. "That's not what woke is. Woke is something very different. It's identity. We see [race] all the time. [Race] is always the most important thing. I don't think that's liberalism."[4]

Others define wokeness as either a subset of or a parallel line of thinking to progressive ideology. To be woke often means seeking evidence of oppression in every imaginable circumstance, and then decrying that oppression through hyperbolic means—racial oppression by lifting up the cause of minorities, sexism by lifting up the cause of women, sexual oppression by lifting up the cause of homosexuals, gender oppression by lifting up the cause of nonbinary and transgender individuals, and so forth.

In many ways, what we think of as wokeness is really the disregard of logic and common sense in order to push progressive social (often socialist) agendas. And for many, unleashing a barrage of accusations seems to be more desirable to them than actually making any sense.

It should be noted that different aspects of the "woke agenda" often intersect, while other parts seem actively opposed. For instance, many who claim to be woke often speak of the evils of the patriarchy and the need to end sexism by fighting for women's rights. Yet these same people also demand that biological males compete in women's sports and undress in women's locker rooms.

In terms of daily practice, much of the practice of wokeness boils down to complaining about perceived injustices—especially complaining by means of social media. For this reason, many view wokeness as nothing more than virtue signaling on steroids.

In my opinion, the common denominator found in most types of woke thinking is the central role of identity in our lives. Wokeness seeks to reduce us to our demographics and nothing more.

Let's explore some of the specific consequences of woke thinking, and how these consequences create a profoundly negative environment for families.

An Overemphasis on Identity

In May 2021, Mayor Lori Lightfoot of Chicago was set to celebrate her second anniversary in office. As part of that celebration, Lightfoot decided to grant several one-on-one interviews to local journalists—a worthy idea for any notable politician.

There was just one problem: for that special one-day opportunity, Lightfoot, who is Black, declared she would only grant interviews to local journalists who were not White.

"The fact is, people in the press corps do not reflect the diversity of the city, and it impacts coverage," Lightfoot said. "When I look out at [the reporters], I see very little diversity . . . it's an embarrassment."[5]

If you think it's an abuse of power for a Black mayor to deny interviews to White journalists—or even a blatant display of racism—you're not alone. The National Association of Black Journalists put out a statement in response to Lightfoot's policy, declaring, "While the mayor has every right to decide how her press efforts will be handled on her anniversary, we must state again, for the record, that NABJ's history of advocacy does not support excluding any bona fide journalists from one-on-one interviews with newsmakers."[6]

Lightfoot's declaration illustrated the same driving principle of wokeness I mentioned earlier—namely, that the core ingredient of woke thinking is the emphasis of identity above all other factors. According to this worldview, your value within society is not determined by what you do (your actions), what you believe (your thoughts), or what you contribute (your purpose). Nor is your intrinsic value based on your status as an individual created in the image of God. Instead, who you are as a human being is boiled down almost exclusively to your demographics—your race, gender, the social class into which you were born, and so on. These unchangeable elements of *you* become the most important part of you by far.

Importantly, all demographic factors are not equal, according to woke thinking. Instead, everything (and everyone) is broken down into two rigid categories: "oppressors" and "victims." In some cases, these categories are defined by numbers. The majority are the oppressors, and the minority are victims. In America, for example, it is now assumed by woke thinkers that White people are inherently oppressive, while minorities are inherently oppressed (and therefore virtuous).

In other cases, the status of "oppressor" or "victim" is based on perceptions of the "haves" and "have-nots." Even though we have roughly an equal number of women and men in our nation, men are categorized as oppressors because they are assumed to have more power than women—an assumption based on the always nebulous invocation of "the patriarchy." Similarly, wealthy people are often considered oppressors who oppose the interests of those who are not wealthy, especially those who are poor.

For these reasons, wokeism can be understood as a subset of Marxism, which reduces entire populations and civilizations to a simplistic rubric of "class warfare."

This exclusive focus on demographics has given rise to the particularly reprehensible acronym DEI—diversity, equity, and inclusion. On the surface, these words sound pleasant; even noble. Indeed, diversity and inclusion are noble goals—when approached organically and with common sense.

Equity, however, is particularly sneaky and sinister. Most people think of equity in terms of equality of opportunity, which has been a hallmark of the American Dream for as long as America has existed. Implicit within that dream is the promise that hard work and dedication will provide opportunity, and opportunity will lead to success. Millions of Americans have walked that path to abundance and prosperity.

In the woke mind, however, equity is always understood as *equality of outcome*—for example, if there are more male science professors than female science professors, it is believed something must be wrong. The only conclusion, then, is that females are being oppressed. Therefore, an outside force—almost always the government or whatever administration is in charge of the organization—must step in and forcibly reconcile the situation by removing male teachers and inserting female teachers in their place. Often this is done regardless of competency, which can be profoundly harmful in the long run.

What is particularly insidious about the woke view of identity is that people are assigned value based on the combined nature of their oppression (or their status as oppressors). We see an unofficial system at work:

- Persons of color have a high value because they are oppressed by White people.
- Women have a high value because they are oppressed by men.
- Members of the LGBTQ+ community have a high value because they are oppressed by those with "traditional" sexuality, who are in the majority.
- Poor people have a high value because they are oppressed by wealthy people. (Or more accurately in America, less rich people are oppressed by those who are more rich.)
- To be White, male, wealthy, straight, or binary results in negative points.

You can see the endgame of this system, especially when point values are combined. According to woke thinking, a female person of color who is gay or nonbinary has automatically been more oppressed than just about every other person in the country, which means such people should be awarded more intrinsic value. Conversely, straight White men are deemed only to be oppressors, which means they carry the least value.

Essentially, the amount of oppression you experience determines the degree to which you deserve to be heard, promoted, or even participate in important elements of society.

Incidentally, this approach may explain why someone like Lori

Lightfoot—who is a gay Black female—could ascend to a high political position while also being an unskillful politician. Throughout her term, Lightfoot was routinely praised by the press and simultaneously abhorred by many of Chicago's residents. Eventually, those residents rose up to make Lightfoot the first elected mayor in Chicago to lose reelection after serving for only a single term.

Perhaps you're thinking, *Why is it a big deal for woke folks to make everything about identity? What's the harm in it?*

The answer is that these viewpoints centering around identity have a direct negative impact on families. Think about the consequences of focusing so doggedly on race, for example. People of color are constantly told they are victims snared in the jaws of systemic racism, oppressed at the hands of White people. White people are told they can't help but be racist and must therefore atone for their sins in some way.

It's impossible to overemphasize racial identity like this without causing racial strife in communities—which is exactly what we have seen happen in the past decade. And, of course, increased racial strife within communities is detrimental to every family that lives in those communities.

The hyperfocus on demographic features is also inherently de-motivational. If the most important thing about me is something I cannot change—my ethnicity, my biology, and the like—then what is the purpose of striving to grow and mature? I will always be a victim or an oppressor. Children who are saturated in that way of thinking will find it difficult to embrace the many opportunities offered by America. Indeed, they may not even recognize these opportunities.

An Overemphasis on Governmental Control

As mentioned earlier, many direct similarities between wokeism and Marxism exist, including the search for class struggles at every strata of society. But the biggest overlap between those systems is the hyperemphasis on governmental authority and control.

For centuries, our nation has debated the merits of "big government" versus "small government." Some believe the federal government should have more control over economic factors or enact a multitude of regulations, while others believe the role of government should be reduced, thereby emphasizing individual freedom. This debate was often couched in terms of states' rights—namely, should the power of governing be primarily seated in federal agencies, or should each state decide the rules and regulations that are appropriate within its borders?

America has nudged back and forth on these issues, with the size of the federal government gradually increasing over time. In spite of disagreements, there has been a fair amount of compromise on both sides.

All of that has changed drastically, however, in recent decades. The size of the federal government has ballooned in extreme ways through several means—federal mandates, executive orders, court decisions, and more. Rarely have these hikes in federal power been initiated by standard legislation as part of a democratic process.

Of course, the government's "land grabs" fit into the socialist agenda quite nicely. Just consider how governmental power has moved beyond political and economic regulation and has now reached its fingers into our communities, businesses, and even homes.

Those types of overreaching used to be resisted or at least resented. But what's different about the woke generation is that so many people now *welcome* increased governmental meddling in their personal lives. Many even *demand* it! Why is this? Because woke thinkers often glorify government as the only solution for society's ills.

Chances are good you have noticed some of these attempts to solve social problems by increasing the size and intrusiveness of the government. The more famous examples include:

- rigging the educational system to saturate children in progressive ideologies.
- requiring religious organizations to provide contraceptive services or pay for abortions.
- attempting to force people to eat healthy foods by adding extra taxes to unhealthy foods or regulating sizes on sugary drinks.
- passing legislation designed to require businesses to increase pay for all workers, or to cover health-insurance costs for part-time employees.
- preventing drilling for oil on both public and private land.

Most recently, one of the greatest examples of trying to use federal authority to solve society's problems took place during the COVID-19 pandemic. For the first time in the history of the United States, the federal government initiated a concerted effort to inject American citizens with an experimental vaccine. In particular, the Biden administration essentially threw out a century of scientific research by ignoring natural immunity and insisting on vaccination as the only tenable solution for the pandemic—a solution that predictably (and catastrophically) failed to contain outbreaks and had the potential to cause a great deal of damage on its own.

As a medical professional, I found it appalling to hear about people being forced to choose between receiving an experimental vaccine and losing their jobs. But woke thinkers loved it. They demanded that government go even further and legally mandate the vaccine, not only for adults, but also for children.

This element of insistence has taken wokeism above the typical "big government" advocates. Woke thinkers' demands for government intervention in the private sphere are couched as an issue of safety. They don't believe regular people are smart enough or informed enough to make decisions for themselves. Therefore, they insist that government step in and enforce their preferences, whether or not private citizens agree.

The same type of thinking applies to any number of issues—gun control, healthcare, social media, private schools, private businesses, and so forth. The woke person consistently insists that government take charge and take control "for the greater good."

These practices are harmful for families because the federal government is a blunt instrument that is not capable of nuance or of determining what is best for individuals or individual families. Therefore, the more that government reaches into private lives and homes, the more damage it does to families.

The Brookings Institution recently released a report on the impact of lockdowns and school closures on children during the pandemic. In the report, the authors noted that after Hurricane Katrina in August 2005, children forced to evacuate their homes for long periods of time suffered a drop of 0.17 standard deviations (SD) in their math scores on standardized tests—a significant loss fortunately limited to a very small percentage of children in a defined geographical area.

By contrast, test results of 5.4 million children throughout the US in the first two years of the pandemic showed that math scores dropped up to .27 standard deviations when compared to overall scores in 2019. Thus, the overall learning disruption caused by COVID-19 lockdown policies was much more severe than what children experienced during Hurricane Katrina—and those difficulties were spread across the nation.[7]

How many tens of thousands of young people suffered severe learning loss because the Centers for Disease Control and Prevention and other government agencies shut down schools? To what degree have we damaged an entire generation of children and their families because we allowed the federal government to defy common sense and enforce regulations that resulted in great harm?

Once again, it's important to note that the federal government and state governments have value. They are significant institutions that play a crucial role in the normal function of our lives. But the more our government reaches deeper into the personal lives of private families, the more our families will experience harm.

An Overemphasis on Restricting Freedom

Let's take a moment to recap. What we often describe as "woke thinking" overlaps in many ways with modern progressive ideologies, which themselves overlap with older socialist ideologies. To a great extent, wokeism *is* based on the philosophy of Marxism as it has come to be expressed in Communism. And as we've seen, Communism has been responsible for right around 100 million deaths across the world in the past century.[8]

One specific element of woke thinking is an overemphasis on *identity* as the most important aspect of people, making individuals definable primarily by means of demographics. Another element of woke thinking is an overdependence on government to solve all problems, which is really a desire to use government to force everyone to adopt woke principles and values.

And all of this leads us to the third overemphasis of woke thinking— namely, that wokeism, along with Communism and modern progressivism, endorses a robust system of censorship as a way of eliminating dissent.

You may have heard protestors or other modern-day thinkers make the claim that "silence is violence." Aside from being a catchy slogan, the idea is that anyone who does not stand up and fight against oppression as defined by woke thinking is guilty of contributing to that oppression. If you are silent about something progressives deem morally wrong, you have contributed to that wrong.

Paradoxically, many woke thinkers also have a lot to say about the violence of speech. According to this way of thinking, if I publicly declare that homosexuality is a sinful practice in the Bible—which is true—then I may cause trauma to people who identify as homosexual. In their minds, this trauma is the same thing as physical violence. In this way, talking or writing about any idea that may potentially offend a person is akin to physically assaulting that person.

For woke thinkers, then, words are dangerous on a physical level—which means people must be protected from potentially harmful words. Which in turn means censorship is a good thing because it prevents harm.

If your head is spinning right now, I get it. That kind of twisted logic makes me want to pull out my hair. But according to woke ideology, censorship of speech can be a noble and valiant goal when doing so helps promote the "correct" way of thinking.

All of this would be mildly amusing if it existed only in the exchange of ideas, but it does not. Many progressive thinkers—and more importantly, many progressive *policy makers*—have dedicated themselves to the elimination of free speech in America. If that sounds hyperbolic, I suggest you have not been paying attention.

One of the more egregious examples in recent years was the short-lived Disinformation Governance Board created by the Biden administration as a subset of the Department of Homeland Security. That board, which was quickly nicknamed the "Ministry of Truth" because of its Orwellian mission, was designed to combat "misinformation" as an arm of the state. Meaning, it would have overseen public discourse in all areas of life with the full might of the federal government. A frightening thought, to be sure!

You have probably heard the terms *disinformation* and *misinformation* quite a lot in recent years. The optimistic definition of these terms is "information that is untrue and harmful to others." In many circumstances, however, what woke thinkers label as disinformation is actually true information they disagree with or ideas they believe will lead to unhealthy ways of thinking or speaking.

As always, the question comes down to this: "Who decides what type of information is harmful?" Or put another way, "who decides what is true or untrue?"

Those questions are best handled in the open by the free exchange of ideas. Smart, healthy citizens can digest information for themselves and make informed choices. But wokeism doesn't desire smart, healthy citizens. Instead, wokeism wants people to be fearful of new information and to simply want to be told what to think, say, and believe.

Another alarming trend in recent years is the collusion between the federal government and the "Big Five" tech companies—Alphabet (Google), Meta (Facebook), Instagram, X (Twitter), and Amazon. On many occasions, those companies were contacted by officials from the Biden administration, who sought to suppress the speech of ordinary citizens, or to even have citizens completely removed from public platforms. In most cases, it seems those companies bowed to federal pressure and complied.

Journalist Matt Taibbi was given a firsthand look at this "censorship industrial complex" when he became part of the team investigating the Twitter files. After purchasing Twitter (now called X), Elon Musk allowed the group to explore the vast vaults of internal communications at Twitter and discover for themselves whether the federal government attempted to interfere with the First Amendment right to free speech.

What they found was chilling—a government-sponsored system of censorship. Here's what Taibbi presented as his opening statement to a congressional committee probing this censorship:

> The original promise of the Internet was that it might democratize the exchange of information globally. A free internet would overwhelm all attempts to control information flow, its very existence a threat to anti-democratic forms of government everywhere.
>
> What we found in the Files was a sweeping effort to reverse that promise and use machine learning and other tools to turn the internet into an instrument of censorship and social control. Unfortunately, our own government appears to be playing a lead role.[9]

Taibbi later added:

> We learned Twitter, Facebook, Google, and other companies developed
> a formal system for taking in moderation "requests" from every corner
> of government: the FBI, DHS, HHS, DOD, the Global Engagement
> Center at State, even the CIA. For every government agency scanning
> Twitter, there were perhaps 20 quasi-private entities doing the same,
> including Stanford's Election Integrity Project, Newsguard, the Global
> Disinformation Index, and others, many taxpayer-funded.
>
> A focus of this growing network is making lists of people whose opin-
> ions, beliefs, associations, or sympathies are deemed to be misinformation,
> disinformation, or malinformation. The latter term is just a euphemism
> for "true but inconvenient."
>
> Plain and simple, the making of such lists is a form of digital
> McCarthyism.[10]

It's hard to understate the threat of these revelations. The First
Amendment is a guaranteed right for Americans. It's part and parcel of
what makes us Americans! Yet our own federal government is attempting
to subvert and even eliminate that right. This isn't science fiction. This
isn't even speculation. Government-sponsored censorship is happening.
These systems were created as a logical next step in woke thinking, and
the danger is colossal if it is allowed to continue. We must work hard at
finding solutions to stem the tide.

As we conclude this chapter, let me state again as clearly as I can that
wokeism is not a silly mode of thinking that will go away if we ignore it
long enough. Instead, wokeism is an ideological descendent of Marxism—
which makes it a clear and present danger to American families.

If any organization has typified wokeism in recent years, I suggest
it is Black Lives Matter, or BLM. As the name implies, BLM displays
the woke obsession with racial identity and racial hierarchies of value,

seeking to elevate the "Black experience" above all other expressions of human life.

For a stretch of several years, Black Lives Matter was ubiquitous in the United States. You saw the slogan at sports stadiums, at schools, on social media profile pics, on corporate presentations, and on flimsy front-yard signs. What you may not know is that BLM functioned in many ways as a modern shakedown machine, seeking donations and "support" from every possible sector of society. Those who refused to fall in line were often branded as bigots, racists, and purveyors of hate. Many companies were threatened with boycotts or financial consequences if they expressed discomfort with the BLM creed.

Another truth you may not be aware of is that Black Lives Matter was founded as a fundamentally Marxist organization. Cofounder Patrisse Cullors has been open about that reality, stating, "The first thing, I think, is that we actually do have an ideological frame. Myself and Alicia [Garza] in particular are trained organizers . . . We are trained Marxists. We are super-versed on, sort of, ideological theories."[11]

Cullors confirmed her Marxist chops by the way she handled the tens of millions of dollars donated to BLM—the organization. A 2021 investigation revealed Cullors had purchased four homes around the country for a total price of close to $3 million. That was in addition to the secret $6 million "Campus" purchased by the BLM organization and used exclusively by its founders.[12]

One of the most striking elements of Marxism at work has always been its hypocrisy. George Orwell's 1945 novel *Animal Farm* includes this sentence that can be applied to Marxist thinking: "All animals are equal but some animals are more equal than others."[13]

From my perspective, however, the most frightening element of the Black Lives Matter movement has been its stated desire to disrupt, and even destroy, the traditional family in America. Here is one of the organization's founding principles: "We disrupt the Western-prescribed nuclear family structure requirement by supporting each other as extended families and 'villages' that collectively care for one another."[14]

Just like other enemies of America, BLM understands that the family—and specifically traditional families—is the cornerstone of America's culture and prosperity. Their desire to disrupt and destroy that foundation should inspire us with all the motivation we need to continue this perilous fight.

SEVEN

CONFUSING GENDER

I was an unhappy girl who needed help. Instead, I was treated like an experiment."[1]

Those are the words of Keira Bell, who was thrust into the public eye in 2021 when she joined a lawsuit against the Tavistock Centre in Great Britain. For many years, Tavistock was one of the world's largest medical facilities focused on "gender-affirming care"—medical interventions of various kinds for women and men (but mostly women) who view themselves as transgender.

Keira's story is not a happy one. Her parents divorced when she was five. Her mother lived on welfare, was an alcoholic, and descended into mental illness of various kinds. Her father, a member of the US Air Force stationed in Britain, was physically and emotionally distant.

Growing up, Keira was a tomboy who enjoyed playing sports and roughhousing with a group of boys in her neighborhood outside of London. Though her home life was in tatters, she took comfort in the stability of her peer group.

All of that changed, however, when Keira hit puberty. She could no longer pass as "one of the boys." She was uncomfortable with her changing body, especially with the bleeding and hormonal shifts brought on by her period. In her own words, "By the time I was 14, I was severely depressed and had given up: I stopped going to school; I stopped going outside. I just stayed in my room, avoiding my mother, playing video games, getting lost in my favorite music, and surfing the internet."[2]

While in this depressive state, Keira was referred to internet communities and groups featuring people who had transitioned—specifically, women who had transitioned into men. This was a new idea for Keira, and it quickly took root. In her mind, this was a way to solve all her problems with a single step—she would become a young man instead of a young woman. She would be welcomed back into the social circles of boys. She would no longer have to deal with the elements of being a woman that felt uncomfortable. She was sold on the promise that *she* could literally become *he*.

Referred to the Gender Identity Development Service at Tavistock when she was just fifteen years old, Keira was diagnosed with gender dysphoria. All of her other symptoms—depression, anxiety, her inability to connect with peers, her insecure attachment with her parents—were ignored. Clinicians made the same promises Keira had made to herself: if she became a boy instead of a girl, all of her problems would be solved.

Doctors gave her puberty blockers at age sixteen, followed by testosterone shots the next year. She grew a beard. Her voice became deeper and more masculine. At the age of twenty, she agreed to a double mastectomy—the surgical removal of her breasts. With all her heart, Keira believed those steps would finally lead to happiness, fulfillment, and peace.

Sadly, they did not. Within five years, Keira began the process of detransitioning. She embraces her identity as a woman once more, yet she lives with many scars—both literal and figurative. It's unlikely she will be physically able to bear children. She has lost her breasts and the ability to breastfeed. Her voice is permanently changed. She has to manage facial hair as a young woman. And she is still navigating a health system that failed in its duty to protect her.[3]

Keira Bell's story is a tragedy. During her most vulnerable years, she was pushed into an inescapable pit by medical professionals who valued an agenda over her life and experiences.

As a medical professional, I am deeply saddened when I read her story. And as a human being, I am deeply angered by the reality that Keira's story is only one among hundreds of thousands of young women and men—even children as young as *three years old*—who have been sold the same lies and "compassionately" shoved over the same cliff.

Remember, those who are actively attacking families in America (and around the world) do so by eroding the basic building blocks of those families. Gender certainly qualifies as a core building block. Therefore, we should not be surprised when we see the rage and confusion generated in today's world around gender realities, sexuality, and the roles of women and men.

In short, gender has become a major part of the war against traditional families. So let's explore three of the major theaters in that war.

Attacks on Biology

For millennia, people have possessed a fundamental understanding of the differences between women and men. Frankly, it has never been difficult to do so, which is one reason our culture's recent struggle with these definitions feels so infuriating.

Progressives in the transgender camp make two specific claims. First, they reject the long-accepted reality that gender exists as a binary— namely, that humans are divided into one of two genders: male and female. Instead, they claim a spectrum broad enough to include a nearly infinite amount of genders. Importantly, human beings have the ability to slide along this spectrum from one side to another, based simply on how they "feel inside."

The second claim is that our physical bodies are completely separated from gender. In fact, it's possible—and perhaps even likely—that a person can be born with a mismatch between their body (i.e., their sexual organs) and their gender. When this happens, it is necessary to undergo a profoundly complicated and hugely expensive series of surgeries in order to correct this biological mismatch.

Do you see the paradox inherent in these two beliefs? On the one hand, those who support a progressive ideology believe gender is so fluid that people can switch back and forth between "feeling male" and "feeling female," based on nothing more than their current emotional state. On the other hand, these same folks tell us gender is so fixed and so vital that surgery is the only option for aligning our emotions with our bodies.

What is particularly galling is the way the transgender crowd loudly and brazenly claims they are "following the science" in supporting such claims. In fact, they—and mainstream media and many politicians and university professors—believe that to question any aspect of these two claims is to reject science itself.

As a decorated doctor and lifelong medical professional, let me set the record straight. In no way does biological science support such claims. Instead, what we see when we study the human body and genetics, and even human behavior, is a clear plan set in place by our loving Creator who created us as "male and female" (Genesis 1:27).

First and foremost, there is a clear, unambiguous difference between an individual with two X chromosomes and an individual with XY chromosomes. The former is female; the latter is male. That reality carries beyond physical appearance and can be traced all the way to our DNA.

Second, the male gamete by itself has twenty-three chromosomes and has no utility for procreation on its own. Male gametes by themselves have no potential to form a human being. Similarly, the female gamete by itself has twenty-three chromosomes and cannot develop into a human being on its own. When these two gametes fuse together, however—when a male sperm fertilizes a female egg—the resulting zygote becomes something completely new. That zygote has forty-six chromosomes and possesses *from the very moment of conception* a complete genetic map and mechanism for its further development.

By week eighteen of pregnancy, the sex of the baby can be determined by ultrasound with greater than 99 percent accuracy. About twenty weeks later, the mother will give birth to a little girl or a little boy. Very rarely is there any confusion about the sex of the baby based on the appearance of external genitalia. Yet even in those rare circumstances when confusion does occur, the baby will grow according to its genetic blueprint, including hormonal influences, and a host of features will reveal its status as male or female.

For example, the pelvis of a female develops in a way that is consistent with the passage of a large head of subsequent offspring through the birth canal. The male pelvis, which is much narrower, develops in a way that facilitates high-speed running. Men generally develop much more upper body strength than do women, although physical power can be more similar when it comes to the lower body.

That is the science. That is the biology. To suggest these factors can be switched around or scaled up or down based on feelings is ridiculous. Even so, many people are advocating this possibility, which is scary. Scarier still is the number of people choosing to believe those suggestions. Studies indicate the number of individuals who identify as transgender have nearly doubled in recent years.[4] Is it possible we are seeing some new development in human history? An update to our genetic code?

By no means. Those same studies show that almost all of the increases are occurring among young people. They are also occurring in specific regions that have a highly progressive bent—New York, Hawaii, California, Washington, DC, Illinois, and so on.[5] In other words, these increases are the result of liberal leaders and policy makers pushing children and teens into relatively unstudied waters.

Remember what Keira Bell said about being treated like an experiment? Hers is not a solitary experience.

I recently saw another shocking news item revealing that members of the Biden administration are proposing regulations that would prevent religious families from adopting or fostering certain youth. Why? Because a family's religious beliefs about biological sex may prevent youth from receiving "gender-affirming care" if they decide they were born in the wrong body and need to transition. In essence, children are being denied full access to some families because of an unscientific philosophy of gender fluidity.[6]

One more thing. Many people see these kinds of trends rising around our world but tend to view them as isolated incidents. They don't want to be pegged as conspiracy theorists if they believe that people, governments, or organizations might actually be trying to harm families.

I understand, but it's crucial to be open-eyed about reality if we are to participate in this perilous fight. We must be willing to call out these attacks when we see them—and not just call them out, but resist them. Make no mistake, traditional families are under attack.

These tactics must stop.

Attacks on Women

As we might expect, the attempt to erode core biological foundations of human life has been harmful to many people, including children and families. But I believe these attacks have been especially destructive toward women.

We don't have space in these pages to explore all of the ways women have been harmed by modern attempts to stoke gender confusion and tension. But I see two specific areas as particularly impactful, especially when it comes to families.

The first is the relatively recent phenomenon of biological males invading (and in many ways threatening to take over) women's spaces in our communities. Because of the inherent physical differences between men and women, it has been vitally important for women to have spaces of their own in public life. This need goes beyond social venues, although those are certainly important. I'm speaking more about spaces that place women in vulnerable situations where they have to worry about the presence of men.

I participated in many contentious congressional hearings during my time at HUD. Yet the most heated one may have been a hearing that focused on access to women's shelters, specifically those designed to house and protect women experiencing homelessness, physical or domestic abuse, drug rehabilitation, and so on.

One lobbying group demanded access to every square inch of those facilities for transgender women—meaning, biological males who identified as women. It didn't matter whether the transgender individuals had undergone any surgical procedures or had just chosen to dress as women. Most of the clients they represented still had male body parts.

Even so, they felt that any person who decided they "felt" like a woman or "identified" as a woman should have access to shelters that were, in many cases, specifically designed to protect women who had been abused by men.

I informed the lobbying group that many shelters contained separate quarters designed specifically for transgender clients. But that feature was unacceptable to them. They believed their clients had to be treated exactly the same as every other woman, or else their rights were being infringed. The fact that their clients were not women—that many or most had penises, for example—did not sway them in the slightest.

In the end, I held fast to my commitment to support the rights of single-sex homeless shelters to accommodate only people whose biological sex matches that of those they serve. I heard from many women in the shelters I visited that they would rather sleep in the woods than be under the same roof as a biological man in their current situation. It was my duty to protect the health and safety of those women, and I did.

How I wish more leaders would do the same!

Of course, I have been labeled a "transphobe" and a "bigot" for that decision and many others. But I understand that derogatory nicknames are part of the price we pay to participate in the perilous fight. Remember, a key element of progressive or woke ideology is the pursuit of censorship—seeking to silence those who disagree with their policies, either through legal means or fear. For that reason, we must never allow ourselves to be intimidated into silence or inaction.

Recent years have also seen a sharp increase in transgender women (biological males) demanding they be allowed to participate in women's sports. We've seen it in some of the "minor" sports such as swimming, cycling, weightlifting, and so on. But it's only a matter of time before biological men seek to dominate sports such as women's soccer, tennis, basketball, and more. That is the direction we are heading.

Let me say once again that the biology on this issue is clear. When it comes to sports, biological men have physical advantages over women that cannot be erased by hormone therapies. Men generally have longer arms and bigger hands, for example. They have larger lungs and greater overall musculature. Those features don't go away when a man lowers his testosterone levels. For that reason, it is physically dangerous for men to participate in women's sports.

Just as important, there is much potential harm in demanding that biological men be allowed access to women's locker rooms before and after these sporting events. Riley Gaines was an accomplished swimmer at the University of Kentucky—a twelve-time All-American. During her senior year, she was forced to compete against Lia Thomas, a six foot four biological male formerly named Will. Ms. Gaines knew beforehand that she would be swimming against Thomas, but she didn't know she would be sharing the same locker room as Thomas. Gaines and the other competitors were shocked and dismayed to walk into the locker room and see Thomas fully naked, with male genitalia entirely exposed.[7]

There is another way gender confusion or gender stereotypes have been used to harm women. Women have been told in many ways that "settling" for the role of wife and mother is shameful—that in order for a woman to have a successful and meaningful life, she must have a successful and meaningful career outside the home.

It's important to recognize that this recent development represents a shift in feminist thinking. The early years of feminism and feminist critique were focused on equality—specifically equality of opportunity. The earliest feminists fought for women to have equal rights, equal opportunities, equal status in society, and equal pay. These were (and still remain) worthy goals.

Newer branches of what some call "radical feminism" have gone further. They believe women will never be fully equal until traditional gender roles are abolished. For this reason, many have sought to demonize the "traditional wife" who stays at home with the children while her husband works outside the home and earns money.

It's easy to see these attempts when you look for them. Women who don't have a career are stigmatized as bound to antiquated values and are "less than" women who work. We see unrelenting pressure from all sides of our entertainment media, which portrays successful women as those who effortlessly balance work and career—or those who abandon family altogether and focus solely on advancements and promotions in the office.

I've heard from many stay-at-home moms about the antagonism that assaults them from every direction. Their work is difficult, yet unappreciated. The many sacrifices they make often go completely unnoticed. Yet consider this: children have significant needs that require a great amount of time and attention. In a situation where both parents work, both parents *should* share between themselves the responsibility to provide for their children's needs. More often than not, however, the bulk of those responsibilities still fall to the mother, who simply doesn't have time to carry them all.

Attacks on Men

If you're like me, you've probably heard a lot about patriarchy in recent years. That term is rarely defined in a meaningful way; rather, it is invoked regularly as a root cause of many ills and inequalities currently plaguing our society.

For that reason, you may be under the impression that men as a whole are doing very well. You may believe that most men are physically fit, emotionally healthy, and enjoying lives bursting with meaning and purpose. And you would be wrong. Most men in American culture are not doing so well. In fact, many men are working through severe struggles of many kinds—and have been for decades.

Richard Reeves is an author and senior fellow at the Brookings Institution in Washington, DC. He is also the father of three sons. For that reason, he spent substantial time in recent years examining the plight of young men in today's world. What he found was discouraging to say the least.

Reeves wrote a book called *Of Boys and Men.* I found his reasons for writing such a book to be especially poignant, including this one:

> First, things are worse than I thought. I knew some of the headlines about boys struggling at school and on campus, men losing ground in the labor market, and fathers losing touch with their children. I thought that perhaps some of these were exaggerated. But the closer I looked, the bleaker the picture became. The gender gap in college degrees awarded is wider today than it was in the early 1970s, but in the opposite direction. The wages of most men are lower today than they were in 1979, while women's wages have risen across the board. One in five fathers are not living with their children. Men account for almost three out of four "deaths of despair," either from a suicide or an overdose.[8]

In a single paragraph, Reeves highlights three critical issues faced by men today. While Reeves seems to consider these issues as random expressions of culture or perhaps a negative consequence of the push for women's rights, I see them as part of the coordinated attack against the family we've been exploring throughout these pages.

Either way, it's helpful to explore these challenges in light of the gender confusion and strife so evident in contemporary society.

First, today's men are under attack when it comes to *education*. This attack begins at the beginning of the educational process and extends through college. In elementary school, for example, little girls today often outpace little boys in the classroom. In fact, little boys often struggle to engage with school in a meaningful way.

There are several possible reasons, but one certainly has to do with the way schools are structured. Classroom time is primarily focused on sitting still, listening quietly, and then talking when appropriate. This is a comfortable setting for many girls. But if you've ever been around young boys—and especially a group of young boys—you know that sitting, listening, being quiet, and following nonverbal social cues are not particularly natural behaviors for them. The structure of classroom life is difficult for boys, which often results in these same boys being labeled as "difficult" or even "unintelligent."

These disadvantages continue to have negative consequences on male educational experiences through high school and college. Prior to COVID-19, about 88 percent of girls graduated high school on time, while only 82 percent of boys did the same. Boys are also referred to special education programs at much higher rates than girls.[9]

The situation is bleaker with respect to the college experience. Back in 1972, men received bachelor's degrees at a rate 13 percent higher than women. This was correctly labeled a crisis at that time, and programs were put in place to help women access opportunities for postsecondary education. In today's world, however, women receive bachelor's degrees at a rate 15 percent higher than men. As you can see, the crisis for young men is now worse than the crisis was for young women in the sixties and seventies.[10] Yet there are no programs in place specifically designed to help men. Instead, our culture remains firmly fixed on promoting women's rights and defeating patriarchy.

This weakening in education has had enormous financial implications for entire generations of men. Reeves notes that the relative wages for most men today are lower than what men were paid in 1979.

The second crucial issue facing men is an overall increase in *mental health challenges*—the experiences of addictions, depression, suicide, and other "diseases of despair." Several truths stand out on this subject:

+ Today's men are far more likely to commit suicide than women.
+ Men are far more likely to commit a homicide or be the victim of a homicide than women.
+ The majority of overdose deaths from substance abuse occur in men.
+ Men are much more likely to become addicts.[11]
+ For these reasons and more, the life expectancy of men is 5.8 years fewer than the life expectancy of women.[12]

Why are men suffering in these ways? One reason is the seemingly incessant attack against maleness and masculinity delivered through our entertainment media, news media, and the educational system. Young men in particular are told that traditionally male traits such as assertiveness, aggressiveness, independence, and a predilection for the physical world (rather than the emotional world) are all examples of "toxic masculinity." Social media is filled with buzzworthy terms such as *mansplaining*, *manspreading*, and, of course, *patriarchy* that implicitly malign men for being men.

In short, modern men have been told from a young age that they are oppressive forces who need to curtail or eliminate large portions of their natural inclinations. Men are scorned for simply being men, and this scorn produces consequences.

Finally, today's men are under attack in regard to the critical issue of *fatherhood*. They have been told over and over that their role in the family is no longer valid and no longer valued.

For thousands of years throughout human history, men carried the burden of provision and protection for their families. Based in part on the reality that males are generally larger and stronger than females, men have traditionally been the ones to leave the home to secure the necessary resources to ensure the health of the home. Men were the hunters, soldiers, and protectors of the home. Even in recent centuries, as national economies became more focused on individual jobs and careers, most of the jobs that required long hours of physical strength and endurance were assumed by men, and most of those jobs were compensated well. Men were able to earn a living by working hard, regardless of other factors.

In recent decades, however, our society has shifted in drastic ways. The most drastic swing, of course, is that a significant number of women have now entered the workforce. Women are no longer financially dependent on men, which is, of course, advantageous for women. At the same time, those blue-collar jobs that used to pay significant wages have become minimized as a result of automation, social pressures, and many other factors. The traditionally male jobs now pay less and are less revered.

Whether or not these changes are positive isn't the point. Instead, we need to take a moment to appreciate the massive nature of those changes. In many ways, society has been upended. Families have been flipped over. And men are being left behind.

What is especially harmful is the continued derision and disconnection experienced by men in their role as fathers. We hear the statistics about fatherlessness in America today, and the message is ominous. According to the US Census Bureau, almost 25 percent of children live without a biological father, stepfather, or adoptive father in the home. That comes out to nearly 18 million children, which is enough little boys and girls to fill up New York City and Los Angeles four times over.[13]

Certainly, there are many fathers who bear the blame for this crisis. There are men who choose to abandon the home and abdicate their responsibility as fathers. Other fathers are separated from their children by prison bars. But it's also true that many fathers feel disconnected from their role in the home because they have been told over and over that fathers don't matter, that women "don't need a man," that it's no longer necessary for men to serve as providers and protectors for their families, and that such traditional structures are another evidence of patriarchy that should be consigned to the dustbin of history.

In short, many fathers feel tentative or unnecessary in their roles as fathers. These feelings can be connected to the increased confusion and strife around gender norms and expectations in our culture.

Without a doubt, this confusion brings harm to American parents and children. Remember, the traditional family is by far the most successful system ever designed for raising healthy and successful adults. When fathers are absent from the home, however, the opposite occurs.

Specifically, children raised without a father in the home are:

+ four times more likely to experience poverty.
+ more likely to go to prison.
+ seven times more likely to become pregnant as a teen (for girls).
+ twice as likely to suffer obesity.
+ twice as likely to drop out of high school.[14]

When fathers are shoved aside, their children suffer. When fathers are belittled or continually criticized, their families suffer. And when families suffer, our communities, cities, and nation suffer. This cycle of suffering is why we must engage in this perilous fight!

I know much of the content of this chapter feels quite bleak. It may seem as though we are fighting an unbeatable foe—that we have no pathway to victory. Thankfully, that is not the case. Progress can be made—and has already been made.

Remember the Tavistock Centre? Because of the efforts of Keira Bell and others, the clinic underwent an independent review in 2020, which found that the Gender and Identity Development Service (GIDS) left young people "at considerable risk" of distress and poor mental health. It also discovered that the GIDS team members were pressured to adopt an "unquestioning affirmative approach."

As a result, GIDS is being shut down as part of the Tavistock Centre. Britain's National Health Service will seek other options for helping children who experience gender dysphoria or other gender issues that will "ensure the holistic needs" of these individuals "are fully met."

Keira Bell expressed satisfaction that the clinic closed down. She said, "Many children will be saved from going down the path that I went down."[15]

Amen and amen.

EIGHT

USURPING PARENTS

Several years ago, one of my sons was interviewed by a news organization regarding his success in the world of finance. The interviewer asked him, "How did you learn to manage money so well?"

My son said, "I had to be really good at finances as a kid because my parents never gave me any money!"

I chuckled when I heard this because his claim was only partially true. Like many families, Candy and I offered our children a healthy allowance each week. But each child's allowance was dependent on successfully completing their assigned chores. Candy and I were concerned about our kids becoming spoiled because they were growing up in an affluent family. We wanted them to understand firsthand the correlation between hard work and success. So we didn't just teach them *about* earning money; we set up systems to *show* them the value of hard work if they wanted money. (Which of course they did.)

I mention that story as just one example of a parent's responsibility to impart critical values to their children. Being a mom or dad is about much more than simply providing a roof over a child's head and offering three square meals a day. Parents are called to be active in determining which values, priorities, and key beliefs will be important for the well-being of their children, and then in devising plans and methods to make sure that transfer is successful.

These ideas are not new. They are basic elements of good parenting.

Here's another example. Our family was vacationing in New Orleans, and our kids—who were quite young at the time—noticed a man on the street begging for money. We were coming out of a grocery store at the time, and my wife decided this would be a good opportunity for a teachable moment.

We spoke with the man for a few minutes. He said he was hungry and had not eaten in several days. He needed some cash to grab a meal. Because we had several bags of groceries with us, we filled an extra bag with basic staples and gave it to the man. He was grateful and thanked us.

We loaded the rest of our groceries into the car and drove away—but only briefly. We took a few minutes to circle around the block, which was a large one, and came back to see what the man did with our gift. Sadly, the man was gone, but we found the bag of groceries in a nearby garbage bin. He had thrown everything away and left to find a more productive spot.

As you might expect, the kids were confused. We explained that some people choose to live as professional panhandlers, earning a reasonably comfortable living by playing on people's sympathies. This man did not need food after all; he just wanted money.

Candy and I were able to use that experience to reinforce the importance of compassion. We affirmed that acting compassionately is always a good impulse, especially as our Creator has commanded us to remember the poor as a way of serving Him.

However, Candy and I also explained that the world is full of schemers who try to take advantage of compassion. For that reason, we must not be naive. We can develop the discernment necessary to be good stewards of the resources God gives us.

Both of those lessons were important to Candy and me. Both were values we wanted to actively build into the lives of our children, so we looked for opportunities to do that in a meaningful way.

What I'm describing here is the necessity of *formation* within a home. Parents have a calling, not just to observe their children growing from one year to the next, but to actively *form* those children—to help them develop and mature into the very best versions of themselves. This kind of formation isn't something that just happens. It must be implemented day in and day out through intentional strategies.

Obviously, much is required for this kind of formation to take place. Parents must know their children. They must understand who their children are, what they do well, where they need to grow, and how to best accomplish that growth. This requires a level of love, care, and attention that cannot be faked. It's hard work, but the results are profoundly positive both inside the home and out in the community.

At the same time, the process of formation requires children to trust their parents. They don't have to understand everything their parents do or the reasons certain rules are in place. But they must believe their parents have their best interests in mind—that their parents genuinely love them, care for them, and are seeking what is best for them.

Those are the crucial bonds that must be present in a home for values to be transferred from one generation to the next—and then that generation to the next, and to the next, and so forth.

Unfortunately, the relationship between parent and child in America is under attack on several fronts. Specifically, this vital bond is being usurped, with several groups attempting to step between parents and children to impart their own values into the lives of the next generation—values that are often directly harmful to our families, our communities, and our nation as a whole.

Let's explore three ways the roles of parents are being usurped in America today.

Usurped by the Educational System

The founders of our nation recognized education as a major component of freedom. In fact, they designed our democratic system around the necessity of education. John Adams, the second president of the United States, wrote about that necessity in a letter to John Jebb back in 1785:

> The Whole People must take upon themselves the Education of the Whole People and must be willing to bear the expenses of it. There should not be a district of one Mile Square without a school in it, not founded by a Charitable individual but maintained at the expense of the People themselves.[1]

Adams's vision wasn't instituted right away, of course. It took time. Still, private education was valued in the earliest days of our nation, and public education began to expand in the 1800s. For most of our history as a nation, there has been strong alignment between parents and schools over the need to develop strong, moral, patriotic citizens.

After World War I, public education became a larger part of our cultural milieu, and it was generally accepted as a force for good. Certainly, some people objected to the federal government's role in educating children, but most people were happy for the opportunities such an education provided to their children. Teachers' unions began with the formation of the National Education Association in 1857 and expanded with the American Federation of Teachers in 1916. But again, at that point, they were relatively benign organizations that genuinely held the best interests of both teachers and students in high esteem.

Things began to change in the 1960s when radical elements joined the ranks, including a number of avowed Marxists. Individuals with a clear agenda to elevate socialism and denigrate America began showing up in classrooms, joining school boards, and running state education departments.

Remember, these steps were a defined part of the socialist agenda during the sixties and seventies—think back to our discussion of W. Cleon Skousen's *The Naked Communist* in chapter 4. Twentieth-century Russian leader Vladimir Lenin identified education as a key method for spreading socialist propaganda: "Give me four years to teach the children, and the seed I have sown will never be uprooted."[2]

Beyond socialism, other idealogues began participating in the educational system with the specific goal of advancing their own agendas. Examples include civil rights activists, feminists, religious figures, progressives, anti-war demonstrators, and more. Each movement saw the education of children as a powerful opportunity to advance their own cause and expand their areas of influence.

My point is this: Prior to World War II, the mission of the educational system was clear and universally understood. Educators were responsible for educating children. They were charged with communicating information in ways young people could understand. In the decades after World War II, however, that mission drifted toward new territory. Educators began to not only educate children but also to *impart critical values* to them—to go beyond information and guide younger generations in the larger issues of culture, morality, and spirituality.

In short, the educational system moved beyond its goal of providing *information* and instead focused on *character formation*.

Whether coincidentally or not, the rise in the educational system's desire to shape the moral virtue of young children occurred just as women were entering the workplace in ever-increasing numbers. In effect, as mothers withdrew from the home to advance their careers, educators stepped in to fill the void in fostering character formation.

The role of parents was usurped, and it is still being usurped by educators and an educational system seeking to remain the primary influence in the lives of each new generation. This is clearly seen when it comes to imparting woke values and the woke agenda we discussed in chapter 6. Many teachers have been outspoken about guiding their students into progressive ways of thinking, using just about any means necessary. Those methods include:

+ displaying Black Lives Matter flags or LGBTQ+ Pride flags in the classroom.
+ prohibiting students from wearing religious or conservative clothing or accessories.
+ requiring students to complete projects or assignments based on a progressive view of the world (for example, "Write an essay explaining how you have encountered White privilege over the course of your life.").
+ teaching progressive views of sexuality as the only rational way to approach sexual education—and denigrating abstinence as a realistic approach to sex before marriage.
+ distributing condoms and other methods of birth control to students.
+ encouraging students to read books that are pornographic in nature—especially books that explore homosexuality, gender fluidity, and so on.
+ pushing for children and teens to receive COVID-19 vaccinations without first seeking parental approval.

Many other examples could be provided. If you think these and other practices aren't taking place in your child's particular school or your community's school system, I suggest you do some digging. Many of these practices are ubiquitous.

Three specific methods of educational overreach have caught my attention in recent years. The first is the substantial number of school systems and educational programs that adopted the 1619 Project as a core element of teaching history to children. If you're not familiar with this program, it was developed by Nikole Hannah-Jones and the *New York Times*. Originally produced as a custom edition of the *New York Times Magazine*, the 1619 Project has also birthed podcasts, articles, a book, and, importantly, a curriculum.

The central thesis of Hannah-Jones's work is that American history truly began in 1619, when the first slave ship arrived on its shores. In its own words, the Project "aims to reframe the country's history by placing the consequences of slavery and the contributions of black Americans at the very center of our national narrative."[3]

One of the central premises of this work is that America's Founding Fathers initiated the Revolutionary War in an effort not to secure freedom but to maintain the practice of slavery. This claim has been widely rebuffed by noted historians, including a prominent professor of history at Northwestern University who was asked to serve as a fact-checker before the material was published. She vigorously disputed the notion that slavery was a major motivation for the American Revolution—and she was vigorously ignored.[4]

In its final form, the 1619 Project largely exists as a Marxist rewriting of American history designed to vilify America as a racist, greedy, destructive force from the time of its inception. In other words, the project is radical philosophy disguised as history. It is an attempt to shape character and impart values, not to provide accurate information. Even so, its curriculum has been distributed to countless educational institutions across our country.

A second method of educational overreach is the blatant attempt by schools and school systems to step between parents and children on the issue of transgenderism. Many schools now feature a closet or other storage space where students can find chest binders, tucking tape, devices that allow women to stand up while urinating, and more. The goal of providing these items is to allow students to function outside of their biological gender.

Shockingly, these items are provided without the consent of parents. In fact, in most circumstances, students are directly encouraged to hide their possession and use of these items from their parents. Educators and administrators will even call students by a different name ("Cindy" instead of "Stephen") in the classroom but use that student's given name when speaking with parents so those parents won't discover that their child is moving toward transitioning.

This is a clear violation of parents' rights and the parental responsibility to impart values to their children. Yet such practices continue.

Beyond taking an active role in pushing children toward transgenderism, teachers, individual schools, and even entire school systems have ramped up their efforts to indoctrinate children with woke beliefs. For example, an Ethnic Studies teacher in Seattle gave students a quiz about "understanding gender versus sex." The quiz included these questions:

+ "All men have penises": true or false?
+ "Only women can get pregnant": true or false?

A young man marked both answers as "true," which are the correct answers. Yet the teacher marked them as incorrect. The boy's mother was furious, telling reporters, "I keep trying to wrap my head around how it is legal to teach inaccurate information and force students to answer against their beliefs or receive negative scores."[5] Do you see the change in mission? Information is no longer a priority; formation is the goal.

Third, school systems have usurped the role of parents by providing counseling services that often steer around parental involvement, consent, or awareness. Of course, schools have employed guidance counselors for decades (with questionable results). But in recent years—and especially since the COVID-19 pandemic—schools and school systems have spent tens of millions of dollars connecting students with telehealth services.

For example, New York City recently signed a $26 million contract with TalkSpace, a telehealth startup, to provide free therapy services to teens aged thirteen to seventeen. Every teen in the city can download an app and connect with licensed therapists by phone, video, or text. No parent required.[6]

These services are currently available to millions of children and teens across the United States. Without question, school systems have inserted themselves between children and parents in an effort to increase their influence on the former and decrease the influence of the latter.

Usurped by the Entertainment System

Try to imagine the following scenario if you can. (I find it difficult to do so.)

A man wearing makeup strides onto the stage in a middle school or high school auditorium. This man is obviously a man, yet his face is painted in a hyperfeminine way. He is dressed in scanty clothes and wears prosthetic breasts. His buttocks are exposed. Once onstage, the man begins dancing in a hypersexualized way as music plays in the background. He prances and gyrates in front of the children, even at times inviting some of the kids to join him onstage and participate in the dance.

It's difficult to understand how any parent could condone their children's attendance at such a spectacle, but it happens. In fact, these types of drag shows occur with great frequency around our nation, especially in larger cities. Sometimes they are sponsored by the schools themselves, while other times they occur at libraries, festivals, community halls, and the like. Sometimes children and teens are enticed to attend these events on their own, while other times they go with their parents. Sadly, such drag shows are not limited to teens. Many schools and library systems sponsor "Drag Queen Story Hours," in which men in drag read stories to elementary-aged children.

What is the goal of such events? To sexualize young children and teens. Full stop. Promoters of these experiences do so with the goal of making children and teens more comfortable with sexual content and sexual situations from a young age. These are the same people who push to have sexually explicit books and magazines placed in school libraries—for the same reasons. They know what they are doing—intentionally corrupting an entire generation with lewd thoughts that may well manifest as lewd actions in the future.

From a medical perspective, my strong opinion is that such efforts constitute child abuse. The same is true for the massive effort underway to convince young children they were born in the wrong body and need to transition to another gender. As human beings, our brains do not fully develop until we are in our twenties. Children simply do not have the mental acuity to understand or process what they are seeing—let alone what they are experiencing. Our culture is pushing our youngest and most vulnerable generation down an inherently dangerous road filled with pain.

Now, as bad as this is, I know many parents who actively resist any effort to lure their child into such situations, which is good. However, those same parents may not realize the destructive nature of content accessed by children right under their parents' noses. What do I mean? I am referring to the hypersexualized, hyperprogressive content produced by our entertainment industry and sent directly to children and teens each and every day.

Pornography is an obvious example, with porn addictions skyrocketing among children and teens over the past decade. But many parents don't realize how sexualized today's movies and TV shows have become—not only in terms of nudity and graphic content, but also in the normalization of sexual conversations and sexual themes. The same is true for many graphic novels and fictional books marketed toward young people. Many video games now contain sex scenes or feature explicitly violent situations. There are even commercials on the airwaves today that likely would have been R-rated two decades ago.

Social media is especially notorious for distributing harmful content to impressionable young minds. Those platforms are built using algorithms that continually feed new content to users, often pushing content with an abundance of views to new audiences. So if a young person begins looking at sexualized images or videos, such as women in bathing suits, the algorithm will direct more of those images into their content feed. It won't stop there though. It will start to drop in more graphic images and videos, propelling that young person down the dark road of addiction.

Social media apps can be especially dangerous because they are not browser-based, which means they can bypass protective filters or blockers used by parents to monitor what their children are viewing. Also, social media adds the element of social pressure. When a significant number of young people get on board with a certain trend, others feel pressured into participating, whether or not they are ready. The phenomenon of sexting is a particularly harmful example that often snares young girls.

All of this material and much more can be accessed through the internet, and it's often accessed anonymously in ways that do not allow parents to track what their children have seen. It is insidious.

What I especially want to point out, however, is that all of these examples of graphic, mature, adult-themed content are not showing up on children's phones, computers, or gaming consoles accidentally. Children are not "stumbling" onto the path of harmful content simply by being on the wrong website at the wrong time.

No, our children are being fed this content. Deliberately. Intentionally. Regularly.

Once again, this agenda involves more than sexuality. Today's media companies intentionally produce content that amplifies the woke, hyperprogressive emphasis on identity and oppression. Male heroes are denigrated, while female heroes are celebrated. Diversity is lifted up as the supreme virtue in any situation and for any team or organization. Capitalism is questioned or rebuked. Government is lauded as the solution to all problems.

Do these themes sound familiar? They should.

Why is this happening? Because entertainment media has a specific goal to participate in the formation of our children. They have messages they want to communicate and ideas they want to generate. They have images and themes they want to put in children's minds. They have a specific agenda to guide and influence children in the direction they want them to go—a direction often contrary to what parents know to be in the best interest of their daughters and sons.

Usurped by Our Government

It was supposed to be a regular Monday for Jeannette Cooper and her daughter Sophia. Jeannette is divorced, and for years had maintained primary custody of Sophia in an agreement with her ex-husband and his new wife. By court arrangement, Jeannette had custody of Sophia for six days and seven nights out of every week. The girl only spent time with her father on Mondays for custodial visits.

On that particular Monday in 2019, Sophia left to be with her father—and never came back. What happened next was a tragedy in every sense of the word.

As it turns out, Sophia had expressed to her stepmother, and later her father, that she was transgender—that she felt like a boy on the inside. She had also expressed these feeling to Jeannette, who was skeptical of Sophia's claims, largely because her daughter had never exhibited any symptoms of gender dysphoria. In fact, Sophia had always behaved in ways that aligned with traditionally feminine roles.

But on that Monday custodial visit, Sophia told her father and stepmother that she felt "unsafe" with her mother because of Jeannette's skepticism—also because of Jeannette's insistence on using Sophia's name (rather than a male substitute). That moment was a turning point for the family. Sophia's father did not bring her back to Jeannette's home. Instead, he and his new wife went to the courts, claiming that Jeannette had neglected and abused the girl. Even after seven months of investigations failed to uncover any evidence of neglect or abuse, Child Protective Services ruled that Sophia would remain in her father's custody.

Jeannette was completely cut off. For more than three years, she only saw her daughter during family therapy sessions—until those too were closed. Now, even though Jeannette lives ten minutes away, she can only communicate with Sophia through US mail.

Through these trials, Jeannette has continually expressed her love for Sophia and her desire to genuinely care for her daughter rather than engage in pretense. "The thing that I am not complying with is this concept that good parenting means that you affirm a child's idea that there is something wrong with them," she says. "I'm not willing to do that."

Jeannette has felt pressured from every side to conform to an agenda she knows has been harmful to her daughter. But so far, she has refused. "They want me to have a certain understanding that there is such a thing as a child who is born transgender, and this is who they are. I don't believe that. My child is a girl, and I won't lie to her or anyone else."[7]

At first glance, it may seem as if stories like these are outliers. It's easy to believe nothing like that could ever happen to us—nothing like that could ever happen in our communities.

Unfortunately, that way of thinking is becoming more naive by the minute. I've already discussed how our government seeks ways to extend its influence and exert greater control in our lives, including reaching deeper and deeper into our families. The issue of transgender children is already proving to be an effective fulcrum for state and local officials to use in that quest for more power.

Not surprisingly, California is leading the charge when it comes to using transgenderism as a tool to erode parents' rights. On May 3, 2023, the California state legislature passed Assembly Bill 957 as an amendment to the Family Code. The original code stated that courts would decide on the best interest of children involved in legal proceedings by examining "the health, safety, and welfare of the child" as part of those proceedings. Fair enough. A child's health, safety, and welfare should be the top priority for any parent, guardian, or legal officer connected to that child.

But here is what AB-957 added to the Family Code: "As used in this paragraph, the health, safety, and welfare of the child includes, among other comprehensive factors, a parent's affirmation of the child's gender identity or gender expression. Affirmation includes a range of actions and will be unique for each child, but in every case must promote the child's overall health and well-being."[8]

In other words, the bill would make it possible for many more parents to become trapped in the miserable vise Jeannette Cooper experienced. In situations where parents believe their children have been lured into the transgender community by peers or officials pushing an agenda, those parents would have to choose between affirming delusions that are harmful to their children or risking the loss of custody of those children altogether. A rock and a hard place.

Fortunately, AB-957 was too radical even for California governor Gavin Newsom, who vetoed the bill in September 2023. Still, the precedent has been set. Similar bills will become law if our nation continues to head in this dangerous direction. Indeed, parents in progressive states such as Washington and Oregon have lost partial or full custody of their children because of concerns with transgenderism. There are also many examples out there of children who have been referred to "gender-affirming care" by a state without the consent—and sometimes without even the awareness—of their parents.

The gauntlet has been thrown down. The federal government is actively using transgenderism to further erode the rights of parents. How will we respond?

Importantly, we need to understand that what's happening is a common Marxist tactic. Remember, socialists and progressives view government as the primary solution to society's problems, which means their goal is to make government the primary influencer and arbitrator of what is acceptable and unacceptable, morally right and morally wrong.

Healthy families will not allow outside influences to disrupt them or remove a parent's responsibility to impart their values to their children. Therefore, government wants to weaken the health of families to further tighten its influence and control in our homes and communities.

COVID-19 is once again an important case study for this topic. Think back to the many instances during the pandemic when parents were pushed, pressured, and sometimes even threatened if they did not toe the vaccination line.

Unvaccinated parents from Los Angeles to Chicago to New York were denied visitation rights with their children. In almost every case, these decisions were made by judges who saw the state as having the primary say in their children's lives rather than the parents—the ones who should have full and final authority.

Do you honestly believe these types of tactics will be used less often in the future? Do you believe there is any chance that local, state, and federal officials will willingly relinquish their authority over individuals and families? Do you think judges and court-appointed officials will recuse themselves from important decisions because parents should rightly be the ones determining the fate and futures of their children?

Straight answer: no. Government does not willingly relinquish authority, influence, or power. As we engage in this perilous fight, then, we must take legal and ethical steps to reestablish the rights of parents and the agency of moms and dads inside the home. If you feel uncertain on how to join the fight on those grounds, be at peace. In the next couple chapters, I will present concrete, practical steps each of us can take to engage in this perilous fight for the sake of our families, our communities, and the future of our great nation.

NINE

FIGHT
for YOUR
FAMILY

It was a cold afternoon in Detroit as my brother and I walked home from school. We were talking together as we stepped into our kitchen—and we were immediately confronted by two surprises.

The first surprise was a strange man sitting at our kitchen table. Not a stranger, per se. Curtis and I had seen him before. He lived on the streets and was often seen begging for food on different corners or camping out in alleyways under a pile of ragged blankets. We'd never had any negative encounters with this man, but to see him surrounded by the familiar confines of our kitchen was jarring.

The second surprise was the delicious smell of hearty, savory, slow-cooked chili, which just happened to be one of my mom's specialties. She stood at the stove with a wooden spoon in her hand, stirring a huge pot. She greeted Curtis and me without mentioning our guest.

Instantly, I understood what was happening. My mother encountered this man as she ran her afternoon errands and evidently decided he needed something to eat, so she brought him home. Without asking any questions, Curtis and I took our seats at the table and made ourselves ready for the feast to come. Our mouths were watering.

Unlike the panhandler my family encountered in New Orleans later in my life, this man was genuinely ravenous. I watched in wonder as he consumed bowl after bowl after bowl, supplementing the chili with pieces of cornbread from a plate at the center of the table. Eventually, after what seemed like hours, he pushed back from the table, laid his arms across his stomach, and had a look of deepest satisfaction on his face.

I genuinely believe he could not have eaten another bite!

As wonderful as that memory is, I remember most the look of serene gratification on my mother's face as she watched her guest eat his fill. If I close my eyes right now, I can still see her standing in front of that stove, radiant with joy.

There were many other incidents like that one during my formative years. Sonya Carson was a deeply compassionate woman. Despite her limited resources, she did everything possible to improve the lives of those in our community who needed help. She was known as someone who genuinely cared about her neighbors.

Perhaps because of that reputation, people often showed up looking for a place to stay the night—a refuge from the cold. Though she had a generous heart, my mother never allowed those individuals to stay with us. She fed them or tended to other needs, but she never provided a bed. As a single mother with two young children, she understood her responsibility to draw protective boundaries around our family and make sure we were safe.

I'm grateful for the way my mother managed our home. Her example taught me the value of compassion, kindness, and grace. Yet her ability to set boundaries showed me the importance of protecting those who are most vulnerable—a pattern I endeavored to emulate in my own home.

There are several ways today's families can benefit from the example of my mother's dual focus when it came to her household—her ability to reach out with kindness even as she stood in front of us children to protect us. We can adopt a similar posture as families in America today—a posture that starts by refusing to be disheartened or discouraged.

Given everything we've studied in these pages so far, it's possible you may feel overwhelmed at the scale and magnitude of the perilous fight currently taking place against American families. When we see the assaults aimed at American families in general—and our families in particular—we may feel helpless and hopeless.

I understand those feelings. I have experienced them myself at different moments of struggle and strife in my own journey. The stakes are high, and the odds don't seem to be even remotely in our favor.

Yet I would encourage you to take heart because we are *not* helpless in this fight. Just as my mother responded with both generosity and firmness, we can too. Compassionate and vigilant. We can live as good neighbors and decent people, even as we take deliberate steps to strengthen our own families.

I've said many times in these pages that the traditional family is the most effective tool for generational success and prosperity ever designed. Of course, no family is perfect, but a home in which both parents love each other, love their children, and in which all members work together for the mutual benefit of the whole is a beautiful picture of what life should be.

In many ways, the family is a microcosm for life as it was meant to be lived.

For that reason, the easiest and most effective step you can take to fight for the family is to pour yourself into loving, serving, and enjoying your own family—and to make that same decision every day. Make your family a foundational priority in your life, and then don't allow anything to push your family out of that coveted spot. Be firm in recognizing the value of your family and in making decisions that increase that value.

If you find yourself outside of the traditional family structure, don't feel bad, don't beat yourself up, and certainly don't throw in the towel. Regardless of your history, there is no limit to the good you can achieve in your family if you set your mind to be a blessing in the lives of those you love most—another lesson I learned from my mother.

It's never too late to take a stand and fight for the good of your family. No matter what situation you find yourself in right now, focusing on several key steps will help you make a positive impact in the perilous fight for your home.

Strengthen Family Bonds

The first step is to do everything possible to strengthen the bonds between the members of your family—the bonds between husband and wife, between parents and children, and between siblings. Yes, even the bonds between extended family such as grandparents and grandchildren, cousins, and so forth.

As I'm sure you've noticed, our culture seems bent on pulling families apart. Some of those methods are intentionally destructive, as we discussed earlier. However, many of the forces causing chaos in our families are simply the consequences of being connected to a chaotic culture.

I think of the tension many parents experience between what's good for their careers and what's good for their families. I think of the vast amount of time and stress it often takes for students (not to mention their parents) to navigate school, homework, peer relationships, and extracurricular activities. I think of the natural push and pull between our desire to be entertained on weeknights (especially after another hard day of working and caring for our children) and our desire to do something more productive.

For these reasons and more, those of us who carry the responsibility of managing a family must take every opportunity to resist those destructive forces—to stand against whatever may be pulling our families apart. Even more, we must intentionally ensure that our family members are connected by strong bonds of love, fellowship, and genuine care.

When our children were young, Candy and I started a tradition of challenging each of our sons to present a little-known fact at the dinner table each evening. Early on, this often felt like a version of show-and-tell from an elementary classroom. But as they grew older, our sons took up the challenge to find something that wasn't common knowledge—something that required a bit of research.

For years, our sons looked forward to their opportunity to present what they had learned. Of course, being boys, they began to compete a bit, each trying to outdo the other in finding the most impressive or most obscure facts. But we were able to keep it fun.

Looking back, that little game was one of those seemingly small details that made a huge difference in the quality of our lives. The boys loved playing that game. Candy and I loved their excitement, and we were pleased at the opportunity to impart the key value of education to our sons. They were pleased by us being pleased, and the whole thing became a virtuous cycle.

I encourage you to develop similar activities in your home. What does your family love to do together? Do more of it. What brings excitement into your home? What elements of your family routine are wholesome and healthy? What can you do to make lifelong positive memories?

I don't know the answers to those questions for your family—but I bet you do. Take the time to implement whatever schedules, programs, priorities, and opportunities will strengthen the bonds in your home.

By the way, don't ignore the simplest options. Research in recent decades suggests tremendous value in families regularly eating meals together. For example, when families eat dinner together multiple times throughout the week, children:

+ have better academic performance.
+ enjoy higher self-esteem.
+ are at lower risk for substance abuse, depression, and obesity.
+ are at lower risk for teen pregnancy.
+ develop better cardiovascular health.
+ develop bigger vocabularies.
+ develop better eating patterns as young adults.[1]

No matter what it takes, find ways to strengthen the bonds of love and fellowship in your family.

Elevate Your Marriage

A second step you can take to fight for your family is to make your marriage a priority. Why is doing this so important? Because it's easy for children to become the main focus in a household, especially in today's culture.

Should kids be a priority within the family? Absolutely. But it's easy to default to children being the *main* priority or even the *only* priority. Husbands and wives can feel left out of each other's orbits, simply doing whatever is necessary to guide the family through the different routines and requirements of each day.

You know how it can go. Drive the kids to school. Work to make a living. Get some healthy meals on the table. Drive the kids to sports practices or band rehearsals or playdates or medical appointments or driving lessons or any other of the hundreds of opportunities we want to give our offspring. Mow the lawn. Trim the garden. Take out the trash. Fold the laundry. Dust the blinds. Read a bedtime story—then another and another and another. Finally, enjoy a few moments of conversation with the love of your life before drifting off to sleep so you have enough energy to start the whole process again in the morning.

Life can be exhausting, and more specifically, family life can be exhausting. But when our marriages suffer, our families will suffer as well. For that reason, it's critical for husbands and wives to maintain their relationship as a critical priority within the home.

What does this look like on a practical level? Date night is a good start. Or morning walks together before the children wake up. Or establishing excitement for the physical intimacy of sex. Or any other way you can find to show love actively and intentionally to your spouse and then receive love from your spouse.

Another way to elevate your marriage is to come to an agreement on your roles as husband and wife. This can be a sticky subject, I know, so let me take a moment to explain.

Today's culture regularly makes the claim that there are no real differences between women and men, which means there are no real differences between husbands and wives in the home. According to our nation's norms, both husbands and wives are responsible for working outside the home to earn a living and then working inside the home to manage chores, cook meals, raise children, and more. Mom and Dad are essentially viewed as interchangeable parts within the system of a home.

We know from chapter 1, however, that such a view does not line up with God's original design for marriage or for the family. Husbands and wives were designed differently in order to fulfill different roles within the home—differences that are meant to be a blessing for all involved. We harm our families when these differences are ignored.

Now, am I suggesting that every American family return to 1950s-era social roles in which most men work outside the home and most women stay inside the home to manage it and raise the children? No. Cultural shifts and contemporary needs may make it necessary for many families to take a different approach. But there is value in the system of the traditional nuclear family, and it can still be an asset to many types of families today.

What I *am* suggesting is that every family set up roles for Mom and Dad that are clearly defined and mutually agreed upon. Those roles should include:

+ Who is responsible for earning income to keep the home running? (If both spouses are responsible, what is the expected split?)
+ Who is primarily responsible for managing the home?
+ Who is primarily responsible for tending the day-to-day needs of the children?
+ Who is primarily responsible for making meals?
+ Who is primarily responsible for cleaning up after meals?
+ How will conflicts be resolved within the home?

+ Who has the primary responsibility for spiritual formation within the home?
+ What other chores are necessary in a typical week, and who will complete them?

These are the types of questions healthy families ask—and answer. Just as importantly, these topics require healthy communication between Mom and Dad throughout a given month, year, and decade. Situations change, which means roles may need to be adapted or adjusted. Communication is the key to making changes before handling roles becomes a problem.

Establish Clear Boundaries

One of the things I appreciate most about the Old Testament is the way God clearly established His expectations for His people. Beginning with the life of the patriarch Abraham, God declared that He would produce a people from Abraham's offspring—the Jewish people. This was to be God's chosen nation, a people set apart for the specific purpose of revealing Him to the rest of the world.

Several generations after Abraham, once God's people had been firmly established, God passed on a clear written record of how He expected them to behave—what we today call the Ten Commandments:

1. Thou shalt have no other gods before me.
2. Thou shalt not make unto thee any graven image.
3. Thou shalt not take the name of the Lord thy God in vain.
4. Remember the sabbath day, to keep it holy.
5. Honor thy father and thy mother.
6. Thou shalt not kill.

7. Thou shalt not commit adultery.

8. Thou should not steal.

9. Thou shalt not bear false witness against thy neighbor.

10. Thou shalt not covet.[2]

God's expectations for His people were clear and concise, and they were inscribed for all to see. Everyone knew what they were supposed to do—and not do. Just as important, everyone understood the consequences for violating any of those commands.

Families can benefit from a similar approach. Every family should have rules, and those rules should be clearly understood by all involved. Even better, those rules should be written down for all to see. Best of all, those rules should be based on God's Word as the moral compass given by God for the benefit of all people.

And of course, those rules should include the consequences that will be incurred for breaking them.

I've had people tell me that taking such an approach is overly oppressive or legalistic, but I strongly disagree. Having clearly established rules is good for children because it gives them confidence to navigate within a known set of boundaries in which they understand what is expected of them and how they can meet those expectations. Similarly, clearly established rules are good for parents because it takes much of the guesswork out of parenting. How frustrating it can be when every parenting decision is a judgment call! That frustration can be mitigated when the rules are written out for all to see. Finally, communities that have easily accessible rules and regulations tend to be safer and more peaceful than those without such boundaries.

For all of these reasons and more, you can greatly bless and strengthen your family when you determine the key rules that will govern your household, write down these rules, display them for all to see, and explain reasonable consequences that will be handed out if they are ignored.

Minimize Outside Influences

So far we have discussed approaches for supporting your family that can be described as "taking the offensive"—establishing healthy bonds in the family, a healthy marriage for Mom and Dad, and healthy rules and expectations for the entire home. These are positive steps that produce positive results.

But there are also steps you can take to fight for your family that fall into the "adopting a defensive" approach—steps that protect your family from assaults designed to harm it. One crucial defensive step is identifying and minimizing the influence of people and organizations outside of your family who seek to slip into your home.

As I mentioned in chapter 4, pornography and other forms of addictive content have reached epidemic levels in America today. Many parents are aware of the broad dangers posed by technology and the internet yet are blind to the specific dangers confronting their own children.

I hope you'll allow me to be blunt in saying that you *must* know what your children are being exposed to on their devices and in your home. In my opinion, this is not an option; it's a must. It is critical to have a good understanding of the websites your children visit, the videos they watch, the content they receive from friends through text messages or other means, the social media apps they use, the games they play, and so on.

Why? Because there are people and organizations who actively want to harm your family and impart their values to your children, and they can receive direct access through the different means identified above. Technology gives them a conduit through which to pursue their goal.

If you don't know what your children are being exposed to or searching for online, you must take steps to find out. Parental control filters and other protective systems can help you gain that information. I also recommend that you have direct conversations with your children. Whatever route you take, it is vital to do everything in your power to prevent outside factors from wreaking havoc in your home.

This principle also applies to the school your children attend. As mentioned in chapter 8, many of these schools have less interest in teaching academic information than they do in character formation—imparting values that may be directly contrary to what you believe and have chosen to pass on to your children.

Talk with your children's teachers. Go to their classrooms at every opportunity—meetings, volunteer occasions, parent-teacher conferences, and the like. Make every effort to attend PTA gatherings or gatherings of similar organizations connected with your school or operating in your community. Check syllabuses. Review homework. Network with other parents.

In short, do everything in your power to know exactly what your children are being exposed to at school.

Then, if you uncover harmful content or hazardous practices, don't be silent about it. Don't assume everything will be okay, because, truth be told, that is an unlikely outcome. Instead, contact the administration. Talk with the teachers involved. Let them know your specific objections and do not allow them to blow you off or push you around. Make demands. Set boundaries. Contact county officials if necessary.

You are responsible for the health and well-being of your children, which means you must take the initiative to defend them from those who would lead them down a destructive path.

If you believe your child's school is a potentially hazardous environment, take the steps necessary to identify other options. Many parents have pulled their children out of public schools and enrolled them in private schools more closely aligned with their values. The costs may be high, but resources and scholarships are available. In Florida, for example, the "Step Up for Students" program covers a good portion of private-school tuition for families.

Homeschooling is another viable option. When you are the primary influence in your child's life both at home and in the classroom, you have ample opportunity to communicate your values and ensure that the foundation is strong for a bright future.

Have Difficult Conversations

"Hey, son, I need to talk with you about something. Let's go to your room."

I've used those words (or similar words) to start numerous conversations during my career as a parent. Each time I addressed one of my sons in that way, I saw a mixture of emotions come over their face. Sometimes they thought they were in trouble, which was often true; sometimes they thought they were being celebrated, which was also often true; and other times they had no idea what I was about to say.

Engaging in meaningful conversations with our children isn't always easy, especially when teens are involved. But if communication is a critical part of marriage, it is equally important in the relationship between parents and children—especially when those conversations are difficult or uncomfortable.

As we've seen, fighting for your family entails setting boundaries and putting protections in place that limit harmful influences inside the walls of your home. Each time you establish such a boundary, you should also have a conversation. Be open and upfront with your children not only about *what* you're doing but *why* you're doing it.

For example:

- When you install a content filter on your child's devices, take time to explain the addictive nature of pornography and the damage it can cause in a person's life and future relationships.
- If your child has any social media apps, download that app and

follow each of their accounts. Make sure to tell them you are doing so and explain your expectations for how they will conduct themselves online.

+ When you draw boundaries that cut across specific forms of entertainment content—such as R-rated movies or TV shows that contain nudity—explain the reasons for those boundaries. Share your desire to protect them from influences that can harm them even if they don't realize the dangers themselves.

+ Be aware of what your children send and receive through text messages and other forms of messaging on social media apps. Proactively talk with your children and explain why you are reviewing their messages.

Being a parent in the modern world also means initiating difficult or uncomfortable conversations around social issues, including sexuality and gender identity. Many parents have asked me, "What is the right age to talk with my kids about sex?" I've actually done a significant amount of research on that topic, and my answer is that our kids will let us know when they've reached the right age by asking us questions. Some children may start asking those questions as early as three years old, while others will be more reserved.

Most genuine questions about sexuality and gender confusion occur when a child hits puberty—a typically confusing time. The best thing parents can be during those years is a reliable source of love, compassion, understanding, and truth.

Early on, it's important to foster an open and honest environment where your children feel comfortable bringing their questions to you. In addition, the way we answer their questions can make a lifelong impression on them. If we answer openly and honestly, they will continue to see us as a safe source of information whenever something stimulates their curiosity. If we evade their questions—or worse, if we respond with anger to their questions—they will go elsewhere whenever they need important information. Do your best to have conversations about sensitive topics before your kids are exposed to them by their friends, teachers, or the things they see on TV.

Finally, many parents wonder what they should do if their child begins to exhibit signs that could be interpreted as evidence of an alternative lifestyle—homosexuality or transgenderism, for example. How should parents respond if they feel troubled by a child's specific actions, behaviors, ways of speaking, and the like?

First and foremost, parents must remember that all children are intensely curious. This is especially true in younger kids, but even teens are still motivated by the thrill of exploration. So don't overact to specific incidents. When a little boy tries on his mother's high heels, he is not displaying signs that he was born in the wrong body and needs to become a female; he's just being curious. The same is true when a girl plays with army figures rather than dolls. Children are typically unaware of and unimpressed by gender stereotypes; they just want to play.

This is also true for things children say. Parents might be concerned if their daughter says, "I'm a boy today," or, "I'll be a daddy when I grow up." Remember that children pretend all the time. They pretend to be puppies or cats. They pretend to be their favorite characters from books or TV shows. They pretend to be other people from school or from their neighborhood. Pretend play is normal and healthy, so I encourage you not to overreact.

One thing that has helped me as a father is to always remember that I am a representative of my heavenly Father. I am a steward of the children and the family He has given me; therefore I must make every effort to watch over these most precious people by emulating God's love, compassion, and care.

TEN

FIGHT
for ALL
FAMILIES

As we've seen throughout these pages, the perilous fight for American families is not new. It's a battle that has been going on for decades, although it has certainly shifted to new levels of intensity over the past five years or so.

One reason many people seem surprised by the outpouring of vitriol against families today (especially traditional families) is that those assaulting the family have remained subtle for so long. They worked in the background at first. They laid elaborate foundations in some of our most important institutions—the educational system, the media, Hollywood, local government, and, finally, national political groups. Their rage simmered below the surface until they sensed the time was ripe to let it loose.

I was first exposed to this battle when I became involved in the political sphere, and it caught me by surprise. During my season as a presidential candidate, I made clear on the debate stage and in various interviews that I intended to advocate for American families—that I was committed to fight back against the assault that even then was picking up steam.

I'm grateful I had the chance to stand for families during my time as secretary at HUD, and I'm proud of what we were able to achieve in those years. For example, we devoted a great deal of energy to making it easier for qualified individuals to obtain FHA home financing. Because of my mother's determination to save up during my earliest years, I know how important housing can be in our culture. In fact, home ownership is the principal mechanism for accumulating wealth in the United States.

For that reason, our team at HUD did everything possible to make home ownership an attainable goal for as many families as possible. I'm especially proud that home ownership in the Black community hit its peak during the Trump administration. We were able to help families in a tangible way.

As we draw toward the end of this book, you may be thinking, *I wish I could make an impact in the fight against American families, but I'm not a politician. I don't have any real influence in the world. What can I possibly do?*

The answer may surprise you. If you want to support American families, you don't need to hold political office, accumulate a huge following on social media, or generate millions of dollars for lobbying groups. You don't have to "go big" to make a real, life-changing difference for families in our nation.

You can make a difference right now, right where you are—starting with your local community and then branching out to the entire nation. I'll show you how in the next few pages.

Join the Fight in Our Communities

I remember being captivated many years ago by a film called *The Bear*. Its approach is quite interesting—the main characters are not people. As the title suggests, the plot follows a young grizzly bear that is orphaned when its mother dies in a rockslide. Through many adventures, the young bear is taken in by an adult male Kodiak bear, with both animals trying to find a way to avoid a trio of human hunters.

In one scene near the end of the movie, the young bear is chased for several minutes by a hungry mountain lion. After running out of places to run, the little bear turns and does its best to roar—a juvenile attempt to frighten a hardened predator. Undeterred by the little bear's ineffective cries, the mountain lion closes in for the kill.

Suddenly, the little bear's attempts to roar change completely. The audience hears a loud, low-pitched rumble that is packed with power. The mountain lion hears it too and stops midstride. Its head pops up and then it turns away quickly, running backward in obvious fright.

At first, the little bear seems pleased by its sudden prowess. But then the camera pans backward, and we see the Kodiak standing on its hind legs behind the little orphan, roaring with unquestionable ferocity.

One thing I've noticed in my observation of families is that children who feel "backed up" by their mother and father develop a strong sense of worth and confidence that will benefit them for a lifetime. Traditional families have a way of instilling security, conviction, and poise in their children—almost as if they were designed to do so!

When children don't have that kind of support, they typically go out in search of someone who provides it for them. The unfortunate reality is that many of those children turn to negative influences as their "backup grizzly." They seek out men who exude strength and power, regardless of whether those men have developed any sort of moral fiber. This is especially true in cities where criminals carry a lot of sway and are viewed as local heroes. Tragically, this was the fate of my two cousins in Boston—Uncle William's boys. Their lives were cut short after being sucked up into the penal system as teens.

Given my family background, I could have followed such a path. Thankfully, I was fortunate enough to encounter several backup grizzlies who were decent men—men who cared about me as a person and wanted to make a positive impact in my life.

One of those mentors was Mr. J, my fifth-grade science teacher. To a fifth-grader, Mr. J was the epitome of cool. He had a red convertible with a white top and a laboratory filled with animals. (That was allowed in those days.) He was the first teacher who saw great potential in me and decided to develop it. Mr. J helped me put together my first rock collection and let me play with the animals in his laboratory. What especially caught my attention was his microscope, which allowed me to discover a whole new world of microorganisms.

Then there was Mr. D, my band teacher. He knew about our family's financial difficulties, so he always helped me out when parents were supposed to purchase supplies. I played the euphonium in high school and was actually quite talented. I was even offered a scholarship to Interlochen, the famous music camp in Michigan. It would have been quite a feather in Mr. D's cap to have one of his students attend Interlochen, but he cautioned me not to accept the invitation.

"Benny, you're going to be a great doctor," he told me. "I don't want you to get distracted." All these years later, I've never forgotten that he cared more about my future than about receiving accolades as a teacher.

Mr. H was another backup grizzly in my life. He was our high school biology teacher, although he didn't get many opportunities to teach. He spent most of his time every day dealing with misbehaving students. He had a somewhat nerdish demeanor that seemed to make it impossible for many students to pay attention.

In any case, Mr. H saw potential in me. He saw that my opportunity to learn in his class was negatively affected by all the chaos, so he hired me as his lab assistant—my first paying job. This gave me the chance to set up laboratory experiments and do a lot of study on my own, which prepared me for college and later for medical school.

We had other helpful grizzlies in our neighborhood, including an old bachelor who lived across the alley from our house. Curtis and I were playing with a BB gun one day when we missed some of the targets we set up. Unbeknownst to us, the BBs went through the screen of this gentleman's back window.

When he figured out what happened, he spoke with our mother. He didn't yell or make accusations; he just stated the facts. Of course, my mother was horrified and offered to pay for his repairs, but he knew about her financial situation. He proposed that Curtis and I do some yard work on his property as a way to make amends. Through that gesture, he taught me the value of respecting property and respecting people. I'll never forget his example of genuine manhood.

Why do I tell these stories? Because they represent the tip of the iceberg when it comes to the things regular people can achieve when they invest themselves in the lives of others in their communities. Teachers, coaches, neighbors—these individuals supported our family when we had nothing to offer in return. They gave of themselves because it was the right thing to do. Without even realizing it, they assumed their role in the perilous fight for American families. And in doing so, they changed not only my life but thousands of other lives through me.

You have the same opportunity. You can invest in the lives of others at church, through local charitable organizations, through sports teams, or simply by getting to know your neighbors. When you see needs to be met, meet them. When you see people who need help, help them. And especially when you see families in danger of succumbing to the relentless assault seeking to destroy them, step in and offer support.

There are also numerous ways to make a more "official" impact in your community through the democratic process. No, you don't have to run for local office—although it is certainly a vehicle through which good people can make a difference. Other avenues can be just as effective.

Remember when I mentioned that enemies of traditional families have spent decades seeking to gain control of school boards, library associations, local newspapers, city councils, and classrooms? Well, there's nothing that requires us to cede that ground for either the present or the future. We can take it back. In fact, if we want to repel this current assault against the family, we *must* take it back.

That's why I was encouraged to see the victory of Glenn Youngkin in the race for governor of Virginia in 2020. In his first bid for public office, Youngkin was seen as a longshot against Terry McAuliffe, an established politician and former governor. This was especially true, given that no

Republican had won a statewide election in Virginia for twelve years. The deck was stacked against him.

What Glenn Youngkin did have on his side, however, was families. Specifically, he appealed to suburban moms and dads who were deeply enraged over decisions at the state and county levels to keep schools closed for an extended time during the COVID-19 pandemic. Despite the spewing of false rhetoric from school boards and teachers unions, those parents knew their children were at very little risk from COVID-19 but at a huge risk of harm from the ever-lengthening closures.

In addition, many of those same parents were furious about the rising levels of woke policies and doctrines in their school systems. They complained about many of the issues already discussed in these pages— the constant race-baiting and racial strife, the pressure to embrace transgenderism despite the complete lack of scientific evidence, the antagonism toward America and religious expression, and the like.

Instead of assuming they were helpless, those parents banded together and fought back. They ran for local office. They showed up en masse at school board meetings and insisted on reading the pornographic material being forced into the hands of their children by school libraries. They protested and raised awareness and support.

Ultimately, they elected Glenn Youngkin as governor of Virginia, and it's been gratifying to see the many ways he has repaid their support by restoring sanity to that state. The same methods can produce success in any community where families take initiative and join together to take their place actively and consistently in this perilous fight.

Join the Fight in Our Nation

It's an unfortunate reality in our world that many people who want to benefit families believe the best way to do so is through government regulations. They want to create new programs, establish new offices, issue new executive orders, and so forth. This approach is a mistake. Why? Because increasing the size of government is almost never the answer to critical problems in society.

I want to say this plainly because it is so important. As we seek to protect and support American families, we must make sure we do not accelerate more government growth and involvement in the process. In the famous words of Ronald Reagan, "I've always felt the nine most terrifying words in the English language are: I'm from the Government, and I'm here to help."[1]

President Donald Trump understood this principle. During the early days of his administration, cabinet secretaries were instructed to eliminate two government regulations for every new regulation put forth. The goal was to cut the amount of bureaucratic red tape in half. At HUD, we were able to beat that ambitious goal by removing more than two thousand regulations and sub-regulations in that department, which greatly expanded our ability to get things done.

What, then, can be done? One answer is for government to function as it was intended—by passing legislation that supports and protects American families, including traditional families. We need appropriate laws that establish these protections for generations.

What follows is a collection of policies that, if enforced, can strengthen families in America. What you and I can do, therefore, is become more familiar with these policies and cast our votes for lawmakers who support these policies. We can also call and write to current legislators and express our desire to see these policies enacted.

In no particular order, I outline six kinds of policies you can support as part of your fight to strengthen American families.

Support Policies That Grow Families Numerically

The first way to support American families is to enact policies that support growth in American families. Of course, growth is important on many levels, but I'm specifically referring to numerical growth. We need more families, and we need larger families.

As mentioned at the beginning of this book, our nation has undergone a dramatic decrease in population over the past fifty years and more. Abortion has undoubtedly been one of the key drivers of that decline. It's hard to grow more families and larger families when millions of babies are murdered in the womb every year.

I'm grateful that in my lifetime I was able to hear these incredible words established by the Supreme Court of the United States: "*Held*: The Constitution does not confer a right to abortion; *Roe* and *Casey* are overruled; and the authority to regulate abortion is returned to the people and their elected representatives."[2]

The Supreme Court's decision in *Dobbs v. Jackson* was a crucial correction to the error of *Roe v. Wade*, and I am certainly grateful for that correction. However, we must not stop there. As the quote above indicates, the battle over the lives of unborn children is not yet finished. Many states have made abortion illegal because of the *Dobbs* decision, yet the practice continues in many more states.

What is needed is legislation that guarantees the right to life for all American citizens, including those still in the womb. Therefore, we must be boldly vocal about saving our fellow human beings through the legislative process. They are counting on us!

Another way to support the growth of families in the United States is to make it easier for eligible families to adopt children when they desire to do so. I understand there are many women and families who get pregnant but prefer not to keep the baby. Yet there are also hundreds of thousands of families in our nation that would like to have children but are unable to do so. Many of these families are interested in adoption.

It would seem natural to connect these two groups. The problem arises in the multitude of bureaucratic regulations surrounding the adoption process—in addition to the huge expense. I recently spoke with a couple who endured an eleven-month adoption process and paid $35,000 so they could provide a home for a baby. That couple is thrilled with the opportunity to care for a child in need, and they would like to adopt again. However, they are still dealing with residual trauma because of the frightfully difficult process they had to navigate to finally welcome the child into their home.

I asked if the process would be easier the second time since the agencies involved already approved them for the first adoption. Their answer was no. They would have to start over at square one if they chose to adopt another baby.

That's the kind of ideological, bureaucratic nonsense Americans face every single day, and they need some relief. We can support families by making the adoption process cheaper and much more streamlined to help healthy families offer their homes to children in need.

Support Policies That Preserve Marriage

In the same way abortion has harmed children in American families, divorce continues to tear at the fabric of the husband-wife relationship. If we want to strengthen and support families in our nation, one of the crucial starting points is to strengthen and support our marriages.

To be clear, I am not advocating for the elimination of divorce. But I do think the processes currently guiding the pursuit of a divorce are too easy and too simplistic. I know from personal experience the numerous negative effects divorce can have on families and children. Therefore, there must be checks and balances in place to minimize and even prevent that harm whenever possible.

At issue specifically is what the court system describes as "no-fault divorce." As the name implies, a no-fault divorce involves one or both parties of a marriage filing for divorce without having to prove that the other party carries blame for the dissolution of the marriage. This is a relatively new practice, having first been established in California in 1969. And it wasn't until 2010 that every US state established provisions for no-fault divorce.[3]

I would argue, however, that there is always fault in divorce. If one party causes harm, there should be penalties for the guilty party reflected in the divorce settlement. And if those penalties are in place, husbands and wives would have greater incentive to resolve their differences rather than pull the rip cord on their marriage.

The reason this matters is that no-fault divorce legally allows marriages to end much more quickly than in previous decades. When there are relatively few legal or financial consequences connected with divorce, it's natural for people to gravitate toward that option when their marriage hits a rough patch. What those people often don't consider, however, is the harm—both present and future—inflicted on their children once a divorce is finalized. For the sake of families, we should enact legislation to remove or radically reduce incidences of no-fault divorce.

Similarly, we should pass laws with real teeth to punish fathers who abandon their children. When my parents got divorced, I was eight years old. That experience crushed me emotionally. I wanted nothing more than reconciliation for my mom and dad. With the benefit of hindsight, I now understand that was never going to happen because my father had another family. He was clearly the culprit in the divorce proceedings, and he was ordered by the courts to pay alimony to my mother for child support.

Sadly, he ignored that order. He contributed nothing toward the financial welfare of his own children. After years of dragging him to court for failure to pay, my mother gave up on the system.

Many men today, as well as some women, who abandon their families face no significant consequences for neglecting their duty to their children. Yet these children must endure a multitude of disadvantages and harmful circumstances heaped on their shoulders. This is a travesty that significantly harms families.

It should be incumbent upon our legislators to pass tougher laws that include penalties for parents who neglect their children, whether through divorce or other means. These laws must include consequences that are severe enough to change behavior.

Finally, in the same way that reducing divorce will help families, so will pursuing ways to promote an increase in the number of marriages. For that reason, we must eliminate anything that even slightly resembles a marriage penalty in our current society. Immediately. That includes regulations requiring partners to pay higher taxes than two individuals with the same income who are not married.

Because children are generally more successful when raised in traditional families, we should do everything possible to encourage healthy marriages, which includes incentivizing families financially.

Support Programs That Encourage and Maintain Traditional Families

As we've seen, we need more mothers to give birth to more children to facilitate an increase in our overall population as a nation. So the idea of having incentives in place for raising children is a good one.

However, we should exercise wisdom to ensure that such benefits are equally distributed to families with mothers who work outside of the home as well as those who work inside the home. In other words, we should not financially punish stay-at-home moms (or stay-at-home dads) for choosing to sacrifice on behalf of their families.

In a similar way, I believe we should stop incentivizing women who give birth to children outside of wedlock. Let me be careful here, because I know this is a controversial topic. I am not saying we should *punish* single mothers for having children outside of marriage. But I do think our current system *pushes* women to make that choice because of financial considerations.

What do I mean? According to the provisions of today's welfare systems, single mothers receive financial support from the government in order to help them provide for themselves and their children. In addition, these women receive an increase in their support whenever they give birth to a new baby. More children equals more welfare.

This is a problem because, as we've already seen, children born out of wedlock are much more likely to experience poverty, commit crimes, become the victims of crimes, and generally struggle over the course of their lives.

Similarly, modern welfare programs base their benefits on the wages earned by each participant. Those who earn less money receive more benefits. That sounds compassionate, but is it? Is it truly helping those enrolled in these programs for the long term? I don't think so.

On a practical level, what motivation does a person have to work harder and strive for a better-paying job if doing so only results in reduced welfare benefits from the government? What motivation does an individual have to get married if doing so only increases the wages of their household, which will then automatically reduce their welfare benefits and any rental support they receive from the government? The answer is zero.

Many of the welfare programs enacted by our government have locked recipients into a cage of dependence from which they can find no escape. We are incentivizing people to raise children outside of traditional families, which means we are pushing parents to make decisions we know will be harmful to their children.

These systems must stop. Not immediately, of course. There would need to be a three-to-five-year waiting period so people can make alternate plans. But there must be a return to positive social pressure for young women and young men to join together in marriage—not only to benefit each other but also to provide a strong pathway toward success for their children.

Finally, a home is a key factor for any family. Therefore, our legislators should put laws in place that make it easier for husbands and wives to purchase their own home as a cornerstone of their family life and financial future.

Speaking of our homes, it's important to see a concerted effort from all three branches of government and the business community to provide working environments that are efficient, yet family-friendly. There is no question that virtual workspaces in the home can be just as effective as workspaces in office buildings. Allowing one of the parents of a nuclear family to use a virtual home office, provided their productivity does not plummet, would go a long way toward strengthening family units. Establishing such policies would allow one parent to be at home with small children, which many studies have shown to be a massive developmental advantage for those children.

Flexible work hours are also helpful, and tax breaks for creative employers who promote policies that enhance family formation and family strength should be considered as well.

When working from home is not an option, flexible childcare solutions should be more readily available. If we truly want to increase birth rates in our nation, we must make life easier for families, not harder. Wise legislators and government officials would do well to study programs that have been successful in other nations and incentivize employers in their sphere to make them available here.

Support a Reduction in the Size of Our Government

Many people are afraid to put on pause, reduce, or even eliminate government financial support for needy communities because they believe these communities have no other option. They think, *If the government doesn't step in to help people in need, who will?*

Interestingly, for the majority of our nation's existence—specifically, before the proliferation of government bureaucratic agencies with huge budgets and minimal oversight—the US relied on a highly effective mechanism when it came to caring for the indigent, the infirmed, orphans, homeless people, and many other people on the margins of society. That system was called the church—or, more accurately, churches.

For much of our nation's history, houses of worship played a key role in our religious expressions, educational systems, and efforts to care for the poor and needy. Religious institutions offered people a direct way to care for others and be involved in the lives of their fellow citizens. And they still do, as long as they are allowed to participate. What many people don't realize is that government programs sometimes step between churches and those they desire to serve. Government programs can hoover up money and other resources that were once distributed—and distributed more effectively, I argue—by churches. After all, these churches, unlike government, are visibly present in the community. They know and understand the needs of their neighbors.

One of the programs we started at HUD was called the Mustard Seed Series. We recognized that churches in needy neighborhoods were perfectly positioned to assess needs and minister to many needy people in their communities. The Mustard Seed Series made it possible for churches to receive government grants to expand their social programs and care approaches for their people. This allowed government to partner with churches rather than see them as a competitor.

We were intentionally selective in the churches we chose to support, expanding those that were well-run rather than pouring resources into those that were failing. We also did not require churches to jump through a bunch of bureaucratic hoops or cut through oodles of red tape. As a result, we saw amazing results.

In general, reducing the size and scope of government will bring power back to local communities when it comes to caring for and supporting those communities. And, just as important, reducing the size and scope of government can put money and resources back into the pockets of families, which will further strengthen those communities and expand those benefits out to the nation.

The COVID-19 pandemic had a major impact on welfare, the distribution of benefits, and the way Americans view work and income. However, many individuals took advantage of unemployment benefits and collected far longer than they should have, creating an attitude of entitlement. As previously stated, hard work is a crux of American history and crucial to the success of traditional families and America as a whole. The Bible says, "If anyone will not work, neither shall he eat" (2 Thessalonians 3:10). Enough said.

I believe work requirements for healthy welfare recipients should be a no-brainer in situations where the government provides financial support in communities. When enacted, such requirements have been highly effective at reducing welfare deception and incentivizing participants to gain new skills and pursue meaningful employment opportunities.

Support the Flourishing of Children

In addition to supporting policies that enhance marriages and spouses, we should do everything we can to benefit the children of those families. Pursuing this goal should include legislation that encourages and empowers school choice.

As we've seen, the COVID-19 pandemic pulled back the curtain to reveal many of the inadequacies of our nation's public school system. Not only are many of our students poorly educated, but they are also indoctrinated with values that are antithetical to the roots of American culture, to faith, and to many families. Fortunately, the exposure of these issues has resulted in an explosion of families choosing private education or homeschooling. That's the good news.

The bad news is that in most of these scenarios, families are forced to bear the brunt of educational alternatives. Actually, it's worse than that—families who choose private education or homeschooling must still pay taxes to support the public education system that failed them. Parents willing to sacrifice for these alternatives do so because they understand the dangers of sending their children into a system that happily misinforms and misdirects their children away from their own values.

School choice legislation would support these families by requiring the government to subsidize private education and homeschool programs. The idea is that a family's tax money should go to support their own individual students rather than unspecified students within their school district. Over time, increased opportunities for private school students and homeschoolers will boost competition with the public school system, which should result in better educational outcomes across the board.

Another step we can take to support families is to back direct legislation that prevents biological men from competing in women's sports and undressing in women's locker rooms. That is a sentence I never expected to write! Yet here we are. When we as a society cannot understand the injustice of allowing people with a natural biological advantage to dominate those without such an advantage, we are in serious trouble.

For most of our nation's history, the transgender population—those genuinely diagnosed with gender dysphoria—represented well under 1 percent of the total population. That number has skyrocketed in recent years. We must remain committed to protecting young girls, teen girls, and women from being forced into harmful and unwanted contact with men.

In the same way, we must adopt binding legislation that stops adults from taking advantage of children's natural curiosity by pushing them to believe they were born in the wrong gender—and then by pushing those same children toward radical, life-changing surgeries. Much of the psychological manipulation of minors that convinces them to abandon their biological gender is done secretly and without the knowledge of the children's parents.

This is wrong. It is criminal. And it must be codified as criminal behavior with real consequences. I truly hope our legislative leaders will have the courage to legally disallow the indoctrination and subsequent physical mutilation of innocent children.

I recently spoke with a good friend, Elaine Beck, who had just returned from spending time in Hungary—a nation that has gone through difficult times over the past century, including a long stint under Communist rule. But those painful experiences helped both the people and the leaders in Hungary make several radical changes for the better.

I listened with growing curiosity as Elaine explained how forcefully Hungary has opposed the indoctrination of little children, especially in terms of transgenderism and LGBTQ+ philosophy. They have passed laws preventing schools and other organizations from pushing children toward gender confusion or sex-change operations. And they have strong prohibitions in place against advertising pornographic materials to anyone under eighteen.

Perhaps most striking of all, the Hungarian parliament recently added an amendment to the nation's Constitution that declares, "Hungary protects the institution of marriage as a community formed by a voluntary decision between a man and a woman and the family as the basis for the nation's survival. The basis of family relationship is marriage and the parent-child relationship. The mother is a woman, the father is a man."[4]

Wow! What a strong and courageous stance.

As you might expect, Hungary has received quite a bit of pushback from other nations and officials in the European Union, but they are standing strong in their commitment to protect families. Responding to criticism, the Hungarian prime minister Viktor Orban said, "Gender propaganda is not just . . . rainbow chatter, but the greatest threat stalking our children. We want our children to be left alone . . . This kind of thing has no place in Hungary, and especially not in our schools."[5]

If only politicians in our nation had the backbone and the political will to take such a stand! (They will do so, of course, if they were to feel the full mandate of the American people.)

Finally, support for students should not end in high school. As we've seen, there are many professors who make no attempt to hide their radical leanings and push woke (socialist) ideologies on their students. In fact, many brag about their socialist affiliations. As a result, large numbers of conservative students feel persecuted into silence regarding their faith and values—and even their appreciation for America.

When this kind of biased education is easily discernible on a college campus, the legislative branch of government should work with the executive branch to withhold federal funding until an atmosphere of tolerance and fairness is restored. While this may seem like a drastic measure, it is less drastic than allowing the persistent indoctrination of the next generations, which can only lead to the destruction of America as we know it.

———

I know this chapter contains a lot of information. Politics and policies are not everyone's cup of tea, but they are a critical part of how our nation functions.

You and I don't write the laws in our nation, but we have influence over those who do. We simply need to unite as Americans and make it plain that we want politicians and policies that support American families. When we join together to make our priorities clear—and when we take the time to vote as informed citizens—we can make a change.

We can do our part in this perilous fight.

EPILOGUE

When I was a kid growing up in Detroit, I was a big fan of the Detroit Tigers. In 1968, they had an incredible team that included the last major league pitcher to win thirty or more games in one season. I loved watching Dennis McLain take the mound.

To a kid following those particular Tigers in that particular season, every game was exciting, and it seemed as though a different hero stepped up every night. The team spirit and camaraderie were outstanding, and they had an electrifying season.

They made it to the baseball playoffs, and as they crept closer and closer to the World Series, the level of excitement in Detroit was unbelievable. After all, the Tigers had not been to the World Series in more than thirty-five years. It was amazing! Sadly, the exhilaration quickly faded into depression as the Tigers went down three games to one against the St. Louis Cardinals. Things were looking grim.

But then it happened. Against all odds, the Tigers won the fifth and sixth games to tie the series at three apiece. Then, in an amazing coup de grace, they won the seventh game.

The city of Detroit, which just a year earlier had been torn apart by racial tension resulting in one of the worst riots the country had ever seen, came together. Everyone was rejoicing, regardless of race. "They" suddenly turned back into "us." It was amazing how a city so divided could so quickly reunite when what united them was greater than what divided them.

What happened? My city came together in celebration of our team's victory. Once that seventh game was won, we saw that *we* were one.

Is this kind of unity and reconciliation between liberals and conservatives, between left wing and right wing, possible in America today? After all, we hold our opinions so strongly. Amid the punditry and rhetoric, is there still a story to unite us? Can we find enough common ground to celebrate a shared victory?

With all my heart, I believe we do. I believe that, when all has been said, and the cameras and microphones have been turned off, we remain the UNITED States of America. We have a shared heritage that has triumphed time and time again against overwhelming odds. We can triumph once again in these perilous times, coming together to show a watching world that the American experiment isn't over—in fact, that its best days are still ahead.

But this won't just happen. We won't simply drift into unity. If we want to come together as neighbors and citizens, it will take all of us. We must remember our story as a nation. We must find ways to forgive past hurts and move beyond ignorance, pettiness, and division. We must find the vibrant and timeless things that unite us, the great truths and values that have been treasured by generations before us—truths that are worthy to pass on to our children and our children's children. We must elevate these above the wounds and lies that divide us.

We must do this even in the midst of the battle. We must do this even though our opponents will be cunning and relentless in their attempts to keep us divided and keep us fighting. We must choose harmony over the "my way or the highway" mindset, and we must be committed to the friction of democracy and the small compromises of preferences that allow for mutual respect and open dialogue in a truly diverse society.

God did not give us these unimaginably sophisticated brains just to hold our ears apart. (You can trust me on that; I'm a neurosurgeon.) We are capable of critical thinking. We have the ability to wrestle with tough questions. We can solve extraordinarily complex problems when we devote sufficient time and energy to that effort. In the face of challenges and complexity, we can think, we can reason, we can examine evidence— and then we can choose what we think is best. Sometimes we can persuade others, and sometimes we can even be persuaded.

All of this commitment to utilize our God-given faculties is good and carries great potential to serve us well as individuals and families. It will help us move forward in our articulation of the significance of the traditional family in our society.

These capabilities were not given solely for the benefit of us as individuals. Instead, we are called to use them for the good of our communities. We can and must shine a bright spotlight on agendas that distort the truth about our families. Yes, we may well encounter tough and angry resistance to reasonable discussion. Yes, we will face new problems for every solution. But that's okay. Our grit, determination, and passion for the truth will bring to the table even those with whom we strongly disagree.

Achieving this will require each of us and all of us, at every level of influence, to speak firmly and kindly and to act with generosity and intention. The spotlight must remain on the needs and reality of the family. This debate needs to be public and long-term. Why? Because the American people are, by and large, perceptive and sensible. When we focus on the real issues, cutting through division and distraction, our nation will show its true strength, which has always rested in its people.

The battle is real. The enemies against us are powerful. To win will take resolve and courage. It will take wisdom and conviction. It will take truth and hard work. It will take all of us, united. But there is no reason that we, the American people, cannot overcome the forces that want to tear us apart—no reason we cannot recognize that there is more that unites us than divides us.

We have an amazing country with an amazing future, if only we summon the courage and make the right decisions that will spur us on to win the perilous fight.

ACKNOWLEDGMENTS

I want to acknowledge and thank my wife, Candy, the incredibly talented staff at the American Cornerstone Institute, and the publisher for their outstanding roles in the production of this work. Most importantly, I thank God for direction.

NOTES

Prologue

1. "Why Family Matters: A Comprehensive Analysis of the Consequences of Family Breakdown," Centre for Social Justice, March 2019, 4, www.centreforsocialjustice.org.uk/wp-content/uploads/2019/04/CSJJ6900-Family-Report-190405-WEB.pdf.
2. "Why Family Matters," 5.
3. Quoted in Caitlin Sica, "The Family: The Building Block of Society and Hope of the World," Life Teen, https://lifeteen.com/family-building-block-society-hope-world, accessed February 16, 2024.
4. "Social and Humanitarian Assistance: The Family—Society's Building Block," Nations Encyclopedia, www.nationsencyclopedia.com/United-Nations/Social-and-Humanitarian-Assistance-THE-FAMILY-SOCIETY-S-BUILDING-BLOCK.html, accessed February 16, 2024.

Introduction

1. Cate Lineberry, "The Story Behind the Star Spangled Banner," *Smithsonian Magazine*, March 1, 2007, www.smithsonianmag.com/history/the-story-behind-the-star-spangled-banner-149220970.

2. Nicholas Kristoff, "'We're No. 28! And Dropping!,'" *New York Times*, September 9, 2020, www.nytimes.com/2020/09/09/opinion/united -states-social-progress.html.

3. Kristoff, "'No. 28!'"

4. Kristoff, "'No. 28!'"

Chapter 1: A Great Design

1. Ron Haskins, "Combating Poverty: Understanding New Challenges for Families," Brookings, June 5, 2012, www.brookings.edu/articles /combating-poverty-understanding-new-challenges-for-families.

2. W. Bradford Wilcox, Robert I. Lerman, and Joseph Price, "Strong Families, Prosperous States: Do Healthy Families Affect the Wealth of States?," American Enterprise Institute, October 19, 2015, www.aei .org/research-products/report/strong-families-prosperous-states.

3. Wilcox, Lerman, and Price, "Strong Families."

4. Melissa Kearney, *The Two-Parent Privilege: How Americans Stopped Getting Married and Started Falling Behind* (Chicago: University of Chicago Press, 2023), x.

5. Kearney, *Two-Parent Privilege*, x.

Chapter 2: Community, Culture, Nation

1. Charles Watkins, "Get to Know the Story Behind Muir's 'The Mountains Are Calling' Quote," *Basin and Range Magazine*, www .thebasinandrange.com/get-know-story-behind-the-muir-mountains -calling-quote, accessed January 11, 2024.

2. "John Muir: A Brief Biography," Sierra Club, https://vault.sierraclub .org/john_muir_exhibit/life/muir_biography.aspx, accessed January 11, 2024.

3. "Quotations from John Muir," Sierra Club, https://vault.sierraclub.org /john_muir_exhibit/writings/favorite_quotations.aspx.

4. "Muir: A Brief Biography."

5. "1960 Census: Supplementary Reports: Marital Status of the Population of the United States, by States: 1960," United States Census Bureau, September 11, 1961, www.census.gov/library/publications /1961/dec/pc-s1-12.html.

6. Rose M. Kreider and Tavia Simmons, "Census 2000 Brief: Marital Status: 2000," United States Census Bureau, October 2003, www .census.gov/library/publications/2003/dec/c2kbr-30.html.

7. "America's Families and Living Arrangements: 2021," United States Census Bureau, November 29, 2021, table A1, www.census.gov/data /tables/2021/demo/families/cps-2021.html.

8. "Parenting in America: The American Family Today," Pew Research Center, December 17, 2015, www.pewresearch.org/social-trends/2015 /12/17/1-the-american-family-today.

9. "U.S. Birth Rate 1950–2024," Macrotrends, www.macrotrends.net /countries/USA/united-states/birth-rate, accessed January 11, 2024.

10. "United States Data and Trends: Abortion Statistics," National Right to Life, https://nrlc.org/uploads/factsheets/FS01AbortionintheUS.pdf, accessed January 11, 2024.

11. Luke Rogers, "U.S. Population Grew 0.1% in 2021, Slowest Rate Since Founding of the Nation," United States Census Bureau, December 21, 2021, www.census.gov/library/stories/2021/12/us-population-grew-in -2021-slowest-rate-since-founding-of-the-nation.html.

12. Kimberly Amadeo, "U.S. Education Rankings Are Falling Behind the Rest of the World," The Balance, March 26, 2023, www.thebalance money.com/the-u-s-is-losing-its-competitive-advantage-3306225.

13. "PISA 2022 Results, Volume 1," Organisation for Economic Cooperation and Development, https://read.oecd-ilibrary.org/view/?ref =1235_1235421-gumq51fbgo&title=PISA-2022-Results-Volume-I, accessed December 19, 2022.

14. Chris Papst, "At 13 Baltimore City High Schools, Zero Students Tested Proficient on 2023 State Math Exam," Fox 45 News,

September 18, 2023, https://foxbaltimore.com/news/project-baltimore /at-13-baltimore-city-high-schools-zero-students-tested-proficient-on -2023-state-math-exam.

15. Alix Martichoux, "Is Crime Going Up in America? Some Types Are, New FBI Data Shows," *The Hill*, October 16, 2023, https://thehill .com/homenews/nexstar_media_wire/4258799-is-crime-going-up-in -america-some-types-are-new-fbi-data-shows.

16. "Declaration of Independence: A Transcription," National Archives, www.archives.gov/founding-docs/declaration-transcript, accessed January 11, 2024.

17. Lee Ohanian, "Why San Francisco Is Nearly the Most Crime-Ridden City in the US," Hoover Institution, November 9, 2021, www.hoover .org/research/why-san-francisco-nearly-most-crime-ridden-city-us.

18. Samantha Delouya, "It's Not Just Crime: What's Really Going on with San Francisco's Shrinking Retail District," CNN, August 30, 2023, www.cnn.com/2023/08/30/business/san-francisco-union-square -retail-closures/index.html.

19. Maryann Jones Thompson, "It's Official: A Quarter Million People Fled the Bay Area Since Covid," *San Francisco Standard*, March 31, 2023, https://sfstandard.com/2023/03/31/san-francisco-bay-area -california-population-decline-census-pandemic-covid.

20. "SAMHSA Announces National Survey on Drug Use and Health (NSDUH) Results Detailing Mental Illness and Substance Use Levels in 2021," U.S. Department of Health and Human Services, January 4, 2023, www.hhs.gov/about/news/2023/01/04/samhsa-announces -national-survey-drug-use-health-results-detailing-mental-illness -substance-use-levels-2021.html.

21. "'Diseases of Despair' Have Soared Over Past Decade in US," BMJ Open, September 11, 2020, www.bmj.com/company/newsroom /diseases-of-despair-have-soared-over-past-decade-in-us.

22. Deidre McPhillips, "More Than 1 in 6 Adults Have Depression as Rates Rise to Record Levels in the US, Survey Finds," CNN, May 17, 2023, www.cnn.com/2023/05/17/health/depression-rates-gallup /index.html.

23. Renee D. Goodwin et al., "Trends in Anxiety among Adults in the United States, 2008–2018: Rapid Increases among Young Adults," *Journal of Psychiatric Research* 130 (November 2020): 441–46, www .ncbi.nlm.nih.gov/pmc/articles/PMC7441973.

Chapter 3: The American Family

1. Sonya Carson, quoting Miller's poem in Ben Carson, *Gifted Hands*, 20th anniversary ed. (Grand Rapids: Zondervan, 2011), 7–8.

2. Exodus 20:3–17 KJV.

Chapter 4: Enemies at the Gates (and Inside)

1. Ronan Bergman and Patrick Kingsley, "How Israel's Feared Security Services Failed to Stop Hamas's Attack," *New York Times*, October 10, 2023, www.nytimes.com/2023/10/10/world/middleeast/israel-gaza -security-failure.html.

2. David Satter, "100 Years of Communism—and 100 Million Dead," *Wall Street Journal*, November 6, 2017, www.wsj.com/articles/100 -years-of-communismand-100-million-dead-1510011810.

3. W. Cleon Skousen, *The Naked Communist: Exposing Communism and Restoring Freedom* (Salt Lake City, UT: Izzard Ink, 2017), 297–328.

4. "Current Communist Goals: Extension of Remarks of Hon. A. S. Herlong Jr. of Florida in the House of Representatives," Congressional Record, Thursday, January 10, 1963, https://cns7prod.s3.amazonaws .com/attachments/communist_goals.pdf.

5. Thomas L. Friedman, *The World Is Flat: A Brief History of the Twenty-First Century* (New York: Macmillan, 2006).

6. Kelsey Koberg, "Teachers Unions Spend Big on Democrats Ahead of Midterm Elections," Fox News, October 26, 2022, www.foxnews.com /media/teachers-unions-spend-big-democrats-ahead-midterm-elections.

7. Felicity Barringer, "The Mainstreaming of Marxism in U.S. Colleges," *New York Times*, October 25, 1989, www.nytimes.com/1989/10/25 /us/education-the-mainstreaming-of-marxism-in-us-colleges.html.

8. John Miltimore and Dan Sanchez, "The *New York Times* Reported 'the Mainstreaming of Marxism in US Colleges' 30 Years Ago. Today, We See the Results," Foundation for Economic Education, September 10, 2020, https://fee.org/articles/the-new-york-times-reported-the-mainstreaming -of-marxism-in-us-colleges-30-years-ago-today-we-see-the-results.

9. Jeffrey M. Jones, "Socialism, Capitalism Ratings in U.S. Unchanged," Gallup, December 6, 2021, https://news.gallup.com/poll/357755 /socialism-capitalism-ratings-unchanged.aspx.

10. Karl Marx and Frederick Engels, *Manifesto of the Communist Party* (1848), 24, www.marxists.org/archive/marx/works/download/pdf /Manifesto.pdf.

11. "New Report Reveals Truths about How Teens Engage with Pornography," Common Sense Media, January 10, 2023, www.commonsense media.org/press-releases/new-report-reveals-truths-about-how-teens -engage-with-pornography.

12. "New Report Reveals Truths."

13. Russ Bynum, Terry Spencer, and Trisha Ahmed, "A White Man Fatally Shoots 3 Black People at a Florida Store in a Hate Crime, Then Kills Himself," AP News, August 26, 2023, https://apnews.com /article/florida-store-shooting-fatalities-b65ecad5f81ac8aa35121507d d4f7dcc.

14. Jimena Tavel, "Prosecutor: White Woman Who Killed Black Neighbor amid Ongoing Feud Won't Face Murder Charge," *Miami Herald*, June 26, 2023, www.miamiherald.com/news/local/crime /article276777871.html.

15. Natalie Neysa Alund and Walker Armstrong, "'I'm Drowning': Black Teen Cried for Help as White Teen Tried to Kill Him, Police Say," *USA Today*, September 11, 2023, www.usatoday.com/story /news/nation/2023/09/11/white-teen-indicted-attempted-murder -massachusetts-racially-motivated/70821226007.

16. Megan Brenan, "Media Confidence in U.S. Matches 2016 Record Low," Gallup, October 19, 2023, https://news.gallup.com/poll/512 861/media-confidence-matches-2016-record-low.aspx.

Chapter 5: Eroding the Foundations of Faith

1. David Zweig, "When a Renegade Church and a Zealous County Health Department Collide," Silent Lunch, March 5, 2023, www .silentlunch.net/p/when-a-renegade-church-and-a-zealous.

2. "Calvary Chapel San Jose Ordered to Pay Santa Clara Co. $1.2M in Covid19 Fines," CBS News, April 13, 2023, www.cbsnews.com /sanfrancisco/news/calvary-chapel-san-jose-vs-santa-clara-county -church-ordered-to-pay-1-2-million-fines; "Santa Clara Judge Denies Motion to Dismiss $2.8M in Covid Violation Fines for San Jose Church," CBS News, February 25, 2022, www.cbsnews.com/san francisco/news/santa-clara-county-superior-court-denies-motion-to -dismiss-2-8-million-in-covid-violation-fines-for-san-jose-church.

3. Ariel Zilber, "Nate Silver Blasts 'Crazy' Covid Lockdowns That Closed Churches, Kept Museums Open," *New York Post*, March 7, 2023, https://nypost.com/2023/03/07/nate-silver-blasts-covid-lock downs-that-closed-churches.

4. "Declaration of Independence: A Transcription," National Archives, www.archives.gov/founding-docs/declaration-transcript, accessed January 11, 2024.

5. "The Bill of Rights: A Transcription," National Archives, www .archives.gov/founding-docs/bill-of-rights-transcript, accessed January 11, 2024.

6. Stephen R. McCullough, "School District of Abington Township v. Schempp," *Britannica*, August 7, 2014, www.britannica.com/topic /School-District-of-Abington-Township-v-Schempp.

7. Exodus 20:3–17 KJV.

8. Tim Walker, "Survey: Alarming Number of Educators May Soon Leave the Profession," *NEA Today*, February 1, 2022, www.nea.org /nea-today/all-news-articles/survey-alarming-number-educators-may -soon-leave-profession.

9. Pete Williams, "In Narrow Ruling, Supreme Court Gives Victory to Baker Who Refused to Make Cake for Gay Couple," NBC News, June 4, 2018, www.nbcnews.com/politics/supreme-court/narrow -ruling-supreme-court-gives-victory-baker-who-refused-make -n872946.

10. Nate Raymond, "Colorado Baker Loses Appeal over Refusal to Make Gender Transition Cake," Reuters, January 26, 2023.

11. "Judiciary Committee Uncovers Multiple FBI Field Offices Coordi- nated to Prepare Anti-Catholic Memo," House of Representatives Judiciary Committee, August 9, 2023, https://judiciary.house.gov /media/press-releases/judiciary-committee-uncovers-multiple-fbi-field -offices-coordinated-prepare.

12. "Modeling the Future of Religion in America: How U.S. Religious Composition Has Changed in Recent Decades," Pew Research Center, September 13, 2022, www.pewresearch.org/religion/2022/09/13/how -u-s-religious-composition-has-changed-in-recent-decades.

13. Jeffrey M. Jones, "U.S. Church Membership Falls Below Majority for First Time," Gallup, March 29, 2021, https://news.gallup.com/poll /341963/church-membership-falls-below-majority-first-time.aspx.

14. Attributed to Brennan Manning in DC Talk's song "What If I Stumble?" See Ben Simpson, "The Ragamuffin Legacy," Relevant, April 16, 2013, https://relevantmagazine.com/faith/ragamuffin-legacy.

15. Judith Schiff, "Resources on Yale History: A Brief History of Yale,"

Yale Library, https://guides.library.yale.edu/yalehistory, accessed January 11, 2024.

Chapter 6: Assaulting Identity

1. Constance Grady, "Chrissy Teigen's Fall from Grace," *Vox*, June 14, 2021, www.vox.com/culture/22451970/chrissy-teigen-courtney -stodden-controversy-explained.

2. Grady, "Chrissy Teigen's Fall."

3. Tristan Wood, "Ben Shapiro Talks CRT, 'Wokeism' during Speech at Florida State," Florida Politics, November 16, 2021, https://florida politics.com/archives/473284-ben-shapiro-talks-crt-wokeism-during -speech-at-florida-state.

4. William Vaillancourt, "Bill Maher Finally Shares His Mind-Bending Definition of 'Woke,'" *Daily Beast*, February 28, 2023, www.thedaily beast.com/bill-maher-shares-definition-of-woke-during-jake-tapper -cnn-interview.

5. Christian Spencer, "Mayor of Chicago Refuses to Give Interviews to White Reporters for One Day in Symbolic Gesture," *The Hill*, May 21, 2021, https://thehill.com/changing-america/respect/diversity -inclusion/554753-mayor-of-chicago-refuses-to-give-interviews-to.

6. Spencer, "Mayor of Chicago."

7. Megan Kuhfeld et al., "The Pandemic Has Had Devastating Impacts on Learning. What Will It Take to Help Students Catch Up?," Brookings Institution, March 3, 2022, www.brookings.edu/articles /the-pandemic-has-had-devastating-impacts-on-learning-what-will-it -take-to-help-students-catch-up.

8. David Satter, "100 Years of Communism—and 100 Million Dead," *Wall Street Journal*, November 6, 2017, www.wsj.com/articles/100 -years-of-communismand-100-million-dead-1510011810.

9. Matt Taibbi, "Hearing on the Weaponization of the Federal Government on the Twitter Files," United States House of Representatives, March 9,

2023, https://judiciary.house.gov/sites/evo-subsites/republicans-judiciary
.house.gov/files/evo-media-document/taibbi-testimony.pdf.

10. Taibbi, "Hearing on the Weaponization."

11. Yaron Steinbuch, "Black Lives Matter Cofounder Describes Herself as 'Trained Marxist,'" *New York Post*, June 25, 2020, https://nypost.com /2020/06/25/blm-co-founder-describes-herself-as-trained-marxist.

12. Sean Campbell, "Black Lives Matter Secretly Bought a $6 Million House," *New York Magazine*, April 4, 2022, https://nymag.com /intelligencer/2022/04/black-lives-matter-6-million-dollar-house.html.

13. George Orwell, *Animal Farm* (New York: Harcourt, Brace, 1946), 51–52.

14. Ellie Krasne, "Black Families Matter," Heritage Foundation, June 29, 2021, www.heritage.org/marriage-and-family/commentary/black -families-matter.

Chapter 7: Confusing Gender

1. Keira Bell, "Keira Bell: My Story," Persuasion, April 7, 2021, www .persuasion.community/p/keira-bell-my-story.

2. Bell, "My Story."

3. Bell, "My Story."

4. Azeen Ghorayshi, "Report Reveals Sharp Rise in Transgender Young People in the U.S.," *New York Times*, June 10, 2022, www.nytimes.com /2022/06/10/science/transgender-teenagers-national-survey.html.

5. Ghorayshi, "Report Reveals Sharp Rise."

6. Elizabeth Elkind, "Jim Banks Unveils Bill to Protect Adoption Rights of Parents Who Want to Raise Kids Based on Biological Sex," Fox News, December 7, 2023, www.foxnews.com/politics/jim-banks -unveils-bill-protect-adoption-rights-parents-who-want-raise-kids -based-biological-sex.

7. Riley Gaines, "Testimony before the House Subcommittee on Health Care and Financial Services: 'The Importance of Protecting Female Athletics and Title IX,'" Independent Women's Forum, December 5,

2023, https://oversight.house.gov/wp-content/uploads/2023/12/Testimony-Gaines.pdf.

8. Richard V. Reeves, *Of Boys and Men: Why the Modern Male Is Struggling, Why It Matters, and What to Do about It* (Washington, D.C.: Brookings Institution Press, 2022), x.

9. Cited in Carolyn Thompson, "Boys Graduate High School at Lower Rates than Girls, with Lifelong Consequences," AP News, October 29, 2023, https://apnews.com/article/high-school-graduation-rate-boys-c7b8dff33221e0ded2d1369397d96455.

10. Richard V. Reeves, "Why Boys and Men?," Of Boys and Men, September 10, 2022, https://ofboysandmen.substack.com/p/why-boys-and-men.

11. Destiny Bezrutczyk, "The Differences in Addiction between Men and Women," Addiction Center, www.addictioncenter.com/addiction/differences-men-women, accessed January 11, 2024.

12. Lisa O'Mary, "'Deaths of Despair' among Men Fueling Life Expectancy Gap," WebMD, November 14, 2023, www.webmd.com/men/news/20231114/deaths-among-men-fueling-life-expectancy-gap.

13. "Statistics Tell the Story: Fathers Matter," Father Absence Statistics, National Fatherhood Initiative, www.fatherhood.org/father-absence-statistic, accessed January 11, 2024.

14. "Statistics Tell the Story."

15. Jasmine Andersson and Andre Rhoden-Paul, "NHS to Close Tavistock Child Gender Identity Clinic," BBC, July 28, 2022, www.bbc.com/news/uk-62335665 (the BBC's social affairs editor Alison Holt provides additional analysis in this article).

Chapter 8: Usurping Parents

1. John Adams, "From John Adams to John Jebb, 10 September 1785," National Archives, https://founders.archives.gov/documents/Adams/06-17-02-0232, accessed January 11, 2024.

2. Matt Beienburg, "Education Is the Engine of Freedom Conservatism," Goldwater Institute, September 14, 2023, www.goldwaterinstitute .org/education-is-the-engine-of-freedom-conservatism.

3. "The 1619 Project," *New York Times Magazine*, August 14, 2019, www .nytimes.com/interactive/2019/08/14/magazine/1619-america-slavery .html.

4. Leslie M. Harris, "I Helped Fact-Check the 1619 Project. The Times Ignored Me," *Politico*, March 6, 2020, www.politico.com/news /magazine/2020/03/06/1619-project-new-york-times-mistake-122248.

5. Nikolas Lanum, "Seattle Student Failed Quiz for Answering 'Only Women Can Get Pregnant;' School Responds," Fox News, December 13, 2023, www.foxnews.com/media/seattle-student-failed -quiz-answering-only-women-can-get-pregnant-school-responds.

6. Jocelyn Gecker, "Lacking Counselors, US Schools Turn to the Booming Business of Online Therapy," AP News, December 3, 2023, https://apnews.com/article/mental-health-counseling-school-hazel-bd7 d650184decd94d4570e9841f1cedb.

7. Kelsey Bolar, "How Gender Ideology Separated a Chicago Mother from Her Daughter," Independent Women's Forum, July 26, 2022, www.iwf.org/2022/07/26/how-gender-ideology-separated-a-chicago -mother-from-her-daughter.

8. "AB-957 Family Law: Gender Identity," California Legislative Information, https://leginfo.legislature.ca.gov/faces/billTextClient .xhtml?bill_id=202320240AB957, accessed January 11, 2024.

Chapter 9: Fight for Your Family

1. "Benefits of Family Dinners," The Family Dinner Project, https://the familydinnerproject.org/about-us/benefits-of-family-dinners, accessed January 11, 2024.

2. Exodus 20:3–17 KJV.

Chapter 10: Fight for All Families

1. "The President's News Conference," Ronald Reagan Presidential Library and Museum, August 12, 1986, www.reaganlibrary.gov /archives/speech/presidents-news-conference-23.

2. "October Term, 2021," Supreme Court of the United States, www .supremecourt.gov/opinions/21pdf/19-1392_6j37.pdf, accessed January 11, 2024.

3. AJ Willingham, "What Is No-Fault Divorce, and Why Do Some Conservatives Want to Get Rid of It?," CNN, November 27, 2023, www.cnn.com/2023/11/27/us/no-fault-divorce-explained-history -wellness-cec/index.html.

4. Glenn T. Stanton, "Hungary's Parliament Adds Legal Recognition of Natural Family to Constitution," *Daily Citizen*, December 18, 2020, https://dailycitizen.focusonthefamily.com/hungarys-parliament-adds -legal-recognition-of-natural-family-to-constitution.

5. Krisztina Than, "Hungary Vows to Fight in EU Court to Defend Anti-LGBT Law," Reuters, March 9, 2023, www.reuters.com/world/europe /hungary-vows-fight-eu-court-defend-anti-lgbt-law-2023-03-09.

Dr. Ben Carson and the American Cornerstone Institute

When Dr. Carson's public service came to an end in January 2021, he had a couple of options. He could head down to Florida, kick his feet up on the beach, and spend the rest of his days enjoying the sunshine on the golf course. Or he could use his gifts to keep fighting for the country he loves so dearly.

When he looked at those options, Dr. Carson knew it wasn't really a choice at all. He cherishes his country, and he is filled with gratitude for the liberty and opportunity it has given him as an inner-city kid raised by a single mother—a kid who went on to become a renowned neuro-surgeon, a presidential candidate, and even a Cabinet Secretary in the United States government. With this spirit of gratitude, Dr. Carson knew he couldn't sit back and let his beloved country fall by the wayside.

Dr. Carson could see where we are going wrong in America today, and how to fix it. Christians and conservatives across America were under attack, including assaults on their families, their values, and their faith. He could see how his life story and the lessons he learned directly related to these pressing problems. He knew he needed to stay in the fight to keep the American Dream alive for future generations as well.

Dr. Carson founded the American Cornerstone Institute with a core group of patriotic staff from the administration to further this mission, based on what he has identified as the "four cornerstones" of American excellence: faith, liberty, community, and life. Under Dr. Carson's leadership, the American Cornerstone Institute works to strengthen the bonds that hold our country together by promoting conservative, commonsense solutions to the issues facing our society.

AMERICAN CORNERSTONE INSTITUTE

Faith. Liberty. Community. Life.

From the Publisher

GREAT BOOKS

ARE EVEN BETTER WHEN THEY'RE SHARED!

Help other readers find this one:

- Post a review at your favorite online bookseller

- Post a picture on a social media account and share why you enjoyed it

- Send a note to a friend who would also love it—or better yet, give them a copy

Thanks for reading!